LO[...]
TR[...] S0-BNZ-575

GLOSSARY

—— of ——

FINANCIAL SERVICES TERMINOLOGY

The Institute
of Financial Education®

111 East Wacker Drive
Chicago, Illinois 60601·4680

COPYRIGHT © 1990 BY THE INSTITUTE OF FINANCIAL EDUCATION
ALL RIGHTS RESERVED. THIS BOOK OR ANY PART THEREOF MAY NOT BE
REPRODUCED WITHOUT WRITTEN PERMISSION OF THE PUBLISHER.

FOURTH EDITION

The material in this publication was believed to be accurate at the time it
was written. Due to the evolving nature of laws and regulations on this
subject, The Institute of Financial Education makes no guarantee as to the
accuracy or completeness of the information contained in this publication.
The material in this book does not purport to be advice. If legal advice or
other specialized services and knowledge are required, readers should
seek a competent professional. Examples, including names and titles, are
purely fictitious and are not intended to represent actual savings institutions nor any real persons, living or dead.

LIBRARY OF CONGRESS CARD CATALOG NUMBER 90-81761
ISBN 0-912857-58-7
PRINTED IN THE UNITED STATES OF AMERICA

Foreword

LONG BEACH BANK
TRAINING DEPARTMENT

The financial services business has undergone dramatic changes since the third edition of *The Glossary of Financial Services Terminology* was published. As a result of the Financial Institutions Reform, Recovery and Enforcement Act of 1989 (FIRREA), the regulatory and supervisory structure for savings institutions has undergone significant changes. Changes such as these are naturally reflected in the vocabulary of the financial institution business. This fourth edition of the *Glossary* presents concise, updated definitions for the vocabulary used by today's savings institution professional.

Many members of the Institute staff were involved in developing this updated edition of the *Glossary*. Ed Rozalewicz, product development specialist, and Bob Klausmeier, senior project manager, organized and directed the project, with administrative assistance from Cynthia Carter, Maeleane Henderson, Beverly Johnson and Sharon Kizlyk. Reviews of the material were provided by Institute staff members Jim Bartley, Kathy Clifford, Chris Ernst, Pat Fiene, Cathie Izor, Dennis Klaeser, Jo Ann Krecker, Diane Lamyotte, Veronica Micklin, Georgeann Oberlin, Diane Prah, Deborah Simmen, Brenda Thunherst and Wanda Zeman, and U.S. League of Savings Institution staff members Tom Thomas, Tom Toman and Charlotte Wilson. Mary Gail Bennett, vice president/director of product development, and Gail Rafter Meneley, senior vice president of The Institute, defined the scope of this *Glossary* revision and supervised its development. Patricia Cronin, editorial coordinator, edited and coordinated the production of this *Glossary*. Julie Beich, design coordinator, designed the book cover under the direction of Janet Hill, design manager, Michael Tapia, design and production manager, and Robert W. Brown, vice president/director of marketing.

The result of this team effort is a useful, up-to-date reference tool for both new and experienced financial institution professionals. The Institute welcomes your comments and suggestions for future editions of the *Glossary*.

Dale C. Bottom
President
The Institute of Financial Education

June 1990
Chicago, IL

Index

A

abstract of title   A condensed history of the title to a designated parcel of land; an actual file containing excerpts from all documents pertaining to the title, and stating all liens, charges or encumbrances affecting the title.

accelerated amortization   The restructuring of an existing mortgage loan for the purpose of shortening the originally agreed upon loan term by increasing the monthly payments.

accelerated depreciation   The method of computing depreciation whereby the depreciation charges are higher in the first years of an asset's life than in succeeding years.

acceleration clause   A clause of a legal contract that states the lender's right to demand full payment of the debt in the event of a default. It may appear on a promissory note, mortgage instrument or security agreement.

accident and health insurance   A type of insurance that provides monthly benefits to the insured. The benefits are paid for a prescribed period of time if the insured loses income because of an accident or illness.

accommodation check   A check or draft drawn by an institution either on itself or on its account at another institution, signed by an authorized officer and payable to a third party designated by the individual requesting the check. It serves many of the purposes of a money order and is also called a bank check. *See also* check.

accounting   The process of systematically identifying, measuring and communicating economic information and presenting this information in periodic, interpretative financial statements and reports.

accounting equation   The basic equation of double-entry accounting that reflects the relationship of assets, liabilities and net worth (i.e., reserves + stockholders' equity + retained earnings). In its simplest form it may be expressed: Assets = Liabilities + Net Worth.

accrual basis accounting   A method of accounting whereby income and expense items are recognized and recorded when income is earned and expense is incurred, regardless of cash receipt or payment. *See also* cash basis accounting.

accrue   The action of increasing or accumulating. It is used in accounting in regard to depreciation, expense, income, interest and other factors.

accrued interest   The interest that has been earned but not received.

ACH   *See* automated clearinghouse.

acquisition credit *See* origination fee.

acquisition loan A loan for the purpose of purchasing raw (bare) land.

actual cash value The replacement cost of real estate at current market value, minus the sum equal to financial depreciation, technological obsolescence and location deterioration.

add-on interest The interest on a loan that is computed by determining the interest charge for the term of the loan and adding that charge to the principal of the loan. The borrower signs a note for principal plus interest, although only principal is disbursed to the borrower.

adjustable rate mortgage (ARM) A type of alternative mortgage loan program in which, by regulation, the interest rate may be adjusted without interest rate limits, and payments may be adjusted as frequently as each month. (Each individual contract, however, may stipulate interest rate limits and frequency of payment adjustments.) The principal loan balance or term of the loan also may be adjusted to reflect the rate change. The purpose of the program is to allow mortgage interest rates to fluctuate with market conditions.

adjusted gross income The gross income less the total allowable adjustments for federal income tax purposes.

adjustment period The time period between one interest rate change and the next for an adjustable rate mortgage.

advance A loan; more specifically, a loan made by a Federal Home Loan Bank to a member institution.

adverse action A denial of credit to an applicant.

aggregate demand An expression of how much output consumers, businesses and governments want to buy at given levels of prices.

agreed order A statement in the reaffirmation agreement that represents a court order; it is signed by the court, the lending institution's attorney and the borrower's attorney. It provides that the institution can repossess the property, that the right of redemption no longer exists and that all interim payments belong to the institution.

air space A two- or three-dimensional space located above ground level. All condominium apartments above the first floor are located in, and represent title to, air space.

allowable contributions A maximum dollar amount a participant can contribute to an IRA or qualified retirement plan during a taxable year. Contributions are deemed allowable if they meet specific rules concerning their composition and timing. The rules governing allowable contributions differ among the various types of IRAs and qualified retirement plans. *See also* excess contribution.

allowable distributions   The withdrawals from IRAs and qualified retirement plans that are not subject to Internal Revenue Service tax penalties. The Internal Revenue Code specifies the minimum age (59½) that participants must reach in order to begin withdrawing, the minimum amounts that participants must withdraw after age 70½ and the purposes for which withdrawals may be made before age 59½. *See also* conduit; direct transfer; lump-sum distribution; period certain; rollover.

amenity   An advantage that adds to the attractiveness of and the pleasure received from a piece of real estate, such as beautiful scenery, the nearness of good public transportation, tennis courts or a swimming pool.

amortization   The repayment of a debt in a specified number of equal periodic installments that include a portion of principal and accrued interest. Most home mortgage loans are fully amortized. *See also* direct reduction; accelerated amortization.

annual percentage rate (APR)   A measure of the cost of credit, expressed as a yearly rate, that relates the amount and timing of value received by the consumer to the amount and timing of payments made. The APR includes the quoted interest rate plus certain service charges and other finance charges associated with the loan.

annual report   A summary, prepared yearly, of a business' financial condition and major accomplishments. Copies of this informational report are distributed to interested parties such as stockholders, managers and customers.

annuity   A guarantee, often made by a life insurance company, to provide an income paid over the lifetime of a person or persons.

annuity certain   The benefits from an annuity contract that are paid over a guaranteed period of time, whether or not the annuitant is living, as in five-year certain or ten-year certain.

appraisal   An estimate of the worth of a piece of property; especially, an estimate of the market value of a piece of real estate by a professional having knowledge of real estate prices and markets. Usually obtained for mortgage underwriting purposes.

appraised equity capital   The difference between the book value and market value of certain savings institution assets, such as land improvements.

appreciation   The increase in value of a material item, especially an increase in market value of real estate.

APR   *See* annual percentage rate.

ARM   *See* adjustable rate mortgage.

articles of incorporation   A document issued by a government giving a corporation the legal right to do business.

assessment **1.** An estimate of the value of a piece of real property for the purpose of levying taxes; also called assessed valuation. **2.** A charge against real property for some local improvement, such as a sewer repair or street paving; also called a special assessment.

asset and liability mix The relationship of total asset value to outstanding debt in an investment portfolio. *See also* net worth.

asset reserves The funds set aside by a depository institution against transaction account and demand deposit balances. Asset reserve requirements are set by the Federal Reserve Bank. *See also* Regulation D; demand deposit; transaction account.

assets A quality or an item of value; what a business owns and what is owed to the business.

assignment The written transfer of some or all ownership rights to real or personal property from one party to another; the transfer may be actual or conditional upon the performance or nonperformance of specified acts by either party to the contract.

assignment of rents A legal document that assigns all rents and income from a property to the mortgagee if a mortgagor defaults.

assumable loan A loan contract that allows for the transfer of the liability from the original borrower to a new owner of the mortgaged property; the ability of a mortgage loan to be taken over by a new borrower.

assumption The transfer of liability on an existing mortgage loan contract from the original borrower to a new owner of the mortgaged property.

assumption statement A statement, drawn up by the financial institution when the assumption of an existing loan is under consideration, showing the current status of the loan account, as well as general information about the amount and due date of the monthly payment and insurance coverage. *See also* assumption.

ATM *See* automated teller machine.

attachment A seizure of defendant's property by court order as security for any judgment the plaintiff may recover in a legal action.

attachment of security interest The acquisition of the secured party's rights in the collateral. In a secured transaction, attachment makes the security interest enforceable against the borrower.

audit An official examination of account records, policies and procedures of an institution to determine fair presentation of financial statements and/or effectiveness of policies and procedures on operating efficiency. May include confirmation of account balances with customers, evaluation of internal controls and testing the accuracy of transactions recording.

automated clearinghouse (ACH)   An organization formed by financial institutions using a computer-based facility to settle automatic payment and deposit transactions among financial institutions in a given geographic area. *See also* clearinghouse.

automated teller machine (ATM)   A device that is similar to a cash dispenser in purpose and operation. However, an ATM performs a full range of transactions, usually including deposits of funds and transfers.

automatic deposit plan   A plan whereby customers arrange for checks, such as Social Security payments or payroll checks, to be sent directly for deposit to their accounts. *See also* direct deposit.

automatic guarantee   A provision of the Veterans Administration under which it will guarantee without prior approval a mortgage loan made by a supervised lender.

B

bad debt reserve   *See* reserve for bad debts.

balance sheet   A financial statement that reports the types and amounts of assets, liabilities and net worth of an entity as of a certain date.

balloon mortgage   A mortgage with periodic installments of principal and interest or interest only; installment payments do not fully amortize the loan. The unpaid principal is due in a lump sum at the end of the term.

bank draft   An order for the payment of money that is drawn by a commercial bank on its account with an out-of-town bank.

bankers' acceptance   A promissory note that is drawn by a corporation to pay for merchandise and on which payment at maturity is guaranteed on the bank's credit standing. It is generally used in foreign trade when buyers and sellers are unfamiliar with one another's financial condition and therefore require a guarantee of payment by a third party known to have a good credit standing.

Banking Act of 1933   The first major banking legislation of the Roosevelt administration. It created the Federal Deposit Insurance Corporation and provided for insurance of deposits at member banks, regulated the operation of banks, limited branch banking and effected other important changes in banking law. Many of its provisions subsequently were amended. Also known as the Glass-Steagall Act.

banking day   A business day on which a depository institution is open for substantially all of its banking activities.

Bank Insurance Fund (BIF)   A fund that insures deposits in Federal Reserve member banks and other qualifying financial institutions and that is administered by the Federal Deposit Insurance Corporation (FDIC). BIF is the subfund of the FDIC that continues the insurance coverage for deposits that, prior to FIRREA, were covered by FDIC insurance. *See also* FDIC; SAIF; FIRREA.

Bank Protection Act of 1968   A federal law authorizing federal regulators to set minimum security standards for financial institutions.

bankruptcy   The legal process in which a person declares his or her inability to pay debts, any available assets are liquidated and the proceeds are distributed among creditors.

Bank Secrecy Act   A federal regulation requiring financial institutions to report same-day cash transactions that appear suspicious or that are in excess of a specified amount (for most institutions, $10,000) on a currency transaction report to the Treasury Department. Typical cash transactions include deposits, withdrawals, check cashing, checks purchased with cash, wire transfers involving cash, and the exchange of both domestic and foreign currency. This currency transaction report is required for said earlier transactions involving one person with one or more cash transactions, or when multiple people transact for one person or account. Also called the Currency and Foreign Transactions Reporting Act. *See also* currency transaction report.

basis points   An investment term that refers to hundredths of 1% yield. Thus, "50 basis points" higher yield is equal to ½% higher yield for a particular investment.

basis price   The price of a security expressed as yield or percentage of return on the investment.

batch processing   A data-processing technique in which a number of similar data or transactions are collected over a period of time and batched for processing as a group.

bear market   A condition of a stock market characterized by a selling trend and declining prices.

bearer bond   *See* coupon bond.

bearer check   A check payable to cash or to the bearer rather than to a specific party.

bellwether stocks   The major stocks, such as IBM and AT&T, that are believed to consistently reflect current trends in the market.

beneficiary   The person designated to receive the benefits accruing from the funds in a trust account or an insurance policy.

beta   A measure of the nondiversifiable or market risk of a particular security that compares the historical returns of the security to the historical returns of the market. A beta of one indicates that the security's returns were equal to the market average. A beta of less than or greater than one indicates that a security returned less than or greater than the market average.

BIF   *See* Bank Insurance Fund.

binder   A written statement binding two parties to an agreement until a formal contract can be executed. A binder is used to secure insurance for a mortgage until a complete policy is issued.

blank endorsement An endorsement consisting only of the endorser's signature written by hand or stamped; designation of the next titleholder and restrictions on the subsequent use of the negotiable instrument are not stated. *See also* conditional endorsement; endorsement; restrictive endorsement; special endorsement.

blanket mortgage loan A loan made to developers or contractors who have purchased a single tract of land for the purpose of dividing it into smaller parcels for sale or development.

blue chip stock The common stock of large, fairly stable companies that have shown consistent earnings and, usually, have long-term growth potential.

board of directors The governing body of an institution; responsible for the direction of policies and for reviewing the objectives and procedures of the organization.

bond An evidence of a debt; the issuer of the bond usually is obligated to pay the bondholder a fixed sum at a stated future date and to pay interest at a specified rate during the life of the bond. Bonds may be issued by corporations, the federal government, and state and local governments.

bond discount The difference between the purchase price and par value of a bond when the par value exceeds the purchase price. *See also* par value.

bond premium The difference between the purchase price and par value of a bond when the par value is less than the purchase price. *See also* par value.

bond rating *See* rating.

book value The value of a business as a whole; comparable to its net worth on a balance sheet.

bookkeeping The recording and posting of transactions and the maintenance of account records reflecting the financial transactions and activities of an institution.

borrower's acceptance A signed statement from the mortgagor, used in construction lending, stating that all work contracted for is in place and of acceptable quality; that is, the contractor has, to the borrower's satisfaction, fully and equitably discharged his or her obligation under the terms of the contract.

branch office An additional office, physically separate from the main office of a savings institution but subject to the main office's direction and control, at which deposits or withdrawals and loan payments may be made.

breakeven analysis A mathematical process used to determine the level of sales or production at which the total costs and total revenue of a business are equal.

bridge loan   **1.** A short-term loan to cover the period of time between the payoff, or end, of one loan and the disbursement, or beginning, of another loan, usually made for investment trading or construction purposes. **2.** A type of housing-related loan made to home buyers who need to borrow for a downpayment on the purchase of a replacement home before the closing sale on their existing home.

broker   A person who acts as an agent for others in selling or buying securities, real estate, insurance, or other services or products.

brokered funds   The savings deposits, in the form of certificates of deposit, that are placed in an institution by a broker acting on behalf of an investor. Fees and commissions are paid to the broker by the savings institution.

budget   A plan for future expenditures and investments over a specified period of time, taking into account projected income and management objectives, as well as the institution's general asset, liability, capital and reserve positions.

building and loan association   *See* savings association.

building code   A set of municipal or state regulations that states the requirements for the construction, maintenance and occupancy of buildings intended to provide for the safety, health and welfare of the public.

bull market   A condition of a stock market characterized by increased buying and rising prices.

buydown   A mortgage agreement in which the lender pledges to make a below-market-rate loan to a borrower in exchange for an interest rate subsidy. The subsidy is provided by a third party, such as a real estate developer.

buy on margin   The purchase of securities using only a specified fraction of the purchase price. The remainder of the funds needed for the purchase is provided by credit extended by the broker to the buyer.

bylaws   The regulations that an institution makes for its own management. In the case of federal institutions, the form and content of the bylaws are prescribed by federal regulatory agencies.

C

call option The option to buy a given amount of a commodity at a specified price during a specified period of time. *See also* put option.

calling officer A financial institution employee who is responsible for going outside the institution to seek and develop new customer affiliations and to maintain current customer affiliations with the institution.

canceled check A check that has been paid by the financial institution on which it was drawn. It is stamped "paid" on the day it is paid and charged to the drawer's account.

cap *See* payment cap.

capacity A borrower's financial ability to repay a loan according to scheduled payments. It is determined by calculating an applicant's total income minus total expenses, usually on a monthly basis.

capital The money and other property owned by a person or corporation, used in the conduct of business.

capitalization **1.** The process of adding uncollected earned interest to the loan balance. Interest is recorded on the date it is earned whether or not it is collected. Some states prohibit the use of interest capitalization. **2.** A method for estimating the present value of future income. **3.** The total value of owners' investments in a business.

capitalization rate The rate of return in appraising, represented by net rental income compared to the market value of a property. It is expressed as a percentage. Could be compared to the comparable rate of return on other kinds of investments of similar risk.

capital gain or capital loss The profit or loss resulting from the sale or exchange of real estate, securities or other capital assets.

capital market A financial market for long-term debt obligations and equity securities.

capital requirements The level or amount of equity, or capital, typically expressed as a percentage of total assets, that regulatory agencies mandate financial institutions to maintain.

capital stock institution *See* stock institution.

carrying charges The part of the finance cost that is charged by most creditors to cover costs incurred by loaning money or extending credit. Billing fees, administrative expenses and bad debt losses are examples.

cash An accounting term that includes cash drawer money, vault cash, petty cash, and demand deposits in commercial banks or regional Federal Home Loan Banks.

cash basis accounting A method of accounting in which income and expense items are recognized and recorded when cash is received or disbursed. *See also* accrual basis accounting.

cash dispenser A self-service device installed by financial institutions to permit customers to withdraw cash at times when branch facilities are closed and at places other than branch facilities. The customer usually activates the machine with a magnetically encoded plastic card, identifies himself or herself with a secret code, and indicates the type of withdrawal and the amount by using push buttons on the keyboard.

cash equivalent A term referring to instruments that are easily converted into cash, such as receivables, U.S. Government Securities, short-term commercial paper, and short-term municipal and corporate bonds and notes.

cash journals The records of original entry that contain a chronological listing of all cash transactions of a firm. One record is kept for cash receipts and another for cash disbursements. *See also* records of original entry.

cash market The market for commodities or securities in which delivery occurs immediately; also called the spot market.

cashier's check A check drawn by a bank on itself, signed by a cashier or other authorized bank officer and payable to a third party named by the customer making the withdrawal.

certificate account A savings account evidenced by a certificate which, if held for a fixed or minimum term, will receive a fixed or variable rate of return greater than a regular savings account.

certificate of compliance A written statement issued by government agencies requesting a customer's financial records; it certifies that the agency complied with the requirements of the Right to Financial Privacy Act to gain access to the records.

certificate of deposit *See* certificate account.

certificate of title The evidence of ownership for an automobile or recreational vehicle. It gives a description of the property and lists any liens against it.

certified check A check that guarantees the following: (1) the signature of the drawer is genuine and (2) sufficient funds are on deposit for its payment. The amount certified is set aside by the financial institution for the express purpose of paying the check, and the financial institution is obligated to pay the check when payment is requested.

certified financial planner   A designation offered by some colleges to individuals who complete a financial curriculum, qualifying examination and term of experience in the financial services business. Certified financial planners provide personal financial planning for individuals.

certified public accountant (CPA)   A designation given to accountants who have passed a qualifying examination and met certain educational and public accounting experiences as set forth by the state licensing authority. CPAs generally are licensed independent accountants who offer professional services to businesses or individuals for a fee.

Chapter 7 bankruptcy   A type of bankruptcy in which the debtor's assets are liquidated and distributed among creditors. Also called straight bankruptcy.

Chapter 11 bankruptcy   A type of bankruptcy in which a borrower's assets are distributed to creditors according to a plan constructed by the borrower or creditors and in which creditors classify their claims in the way most beneficial to them.

Chapter 13 bankruptcy   A type of bankruptcy in which a debtor proposes a method for partially or wholly repaying debts while retaining use of the assets.

chart of accounts   A listing of the accounts to use in the course of business and a listing of the account numbers to be used in conjunction with account titles.

charter   The legal authorization, granted by the federal government or a state government, for a savings institution or other corporation to do business.

chattel mortgage   A mortgage on personal property, such as an automobile or furniture, given as security for the payment of an obligation.

check   A written unconditional order to a drawee institution to pay out a definite sum of money from the maker's account. *See also* accommodation check; cashier's check; traveler's check.

check collection system   The network of banks, clearinghouses and Federal Reserve Banks with check processing facilities that routes a check from the financial institution where it is first deposited to the financial institution on which it is drawn and, in the process, causes funds to be transferred from the payer's account to the payee's account.

check credit   A line of credit on which customers can write checks to access a preapproved loan amount. *See also* overdraft protection.

check truncation   The process of microfilming customers' paid checks or drafts in which the microfilm is the official record of the transaction. The official record is retained by the customer's institution, and canceled checks and drafts are not returned to account holders.

checking account   *See* demand deposit; NOW account.

classification of accounts   A list of general ledger accounts that provides for the systematic groupings of similar accounts. The classification consists of six major account groups: asset, liability, reserve, capital, income and expense accounts.

clearinghouse   An organization of financial institutions formed to exchange and settle for checks drawn on each other. *See also* automated clearinghouse.

closed-end credit   A type of credit whereby the specific amount of credit to be extended, length of time for repayment and payment amounts are determined before purchase.

closed-end investment company   An investment company that has a fixed number of shares outstanding, with no continuous offering or redemption of shares. The company invests its funds in securities, other corporations or governmental bodies.

closing costs   The expenses that are paid by a buyer and seller for the purchase, sale or financing of a property. These include loan fees, title fees, appraisal fees and others.

club account   A deposit account characterized by small, fixed, weekly or biweekly deposits, a short term and a definite goal for saving. Examples are Christmas club accounts and vacation club accounts.

CMO   *See* collateralized mortgage obligation.

CMSA   *See* consolidated metropolitan statistical area.

collateral   An item, of tangible or intangible value, that is owned or being purchased and that is used to secure promise of future payments. Examples are an automobile, real estate, deposit account or negotiable instrument. A lender can repossess collateral if the loan is not repaid.

collateral loan   A loan for which the borrower has pledged certain property as security for the payment of an obligation.

collateral pledge   The agreement under which a third party pledges a deposit account or other property as additional security for the lender's mortgage-secured advance of funds to a borrower.

collateralized mortgage obligation (CMO)   A mortgage-backed security that passes borrower payments into a trusteed pool from which principal and interest are paid to security holders class by class, with one class completely paid off before any principal is repaid to the next greater maturity class. *See also* real estate mortgage investment conduit.

collection   The actions taken by a lender to contact delinquent borrowers to establish the lender's firm position in dealing with delinquency and to relay a sense of urgency to the borrowers about submitting the past due amount.

combination loans The loans made on unimproved real estate, development loans, and loans on other improved real estate that are combined with permanent financing loans or are made to borrowers who have secured permanent financing from other lenders.

commercial bank A privately owned and operated financial institution chartered by a state or federal agency for the purposes of facilitating commerce, providing a safe repository for deposited funds, facilitating the transfer of those funds by check and extending credit.

commercial loan A loan for the purpose of financing inventory or operating expenses of a business.

commercial mortgage loan A loan secured by real estate. The real estate is used for business purposes or to generate income. Also known as income property loan.

commercial paper An unsecured promissory note issued by a corporation at a discount from face value; it is to be redeemed in a short period of time, usually 90 days. Exempt from SEC registration when maturity is under 270 days.

commission The compensation paid to a person for transacting some business or doing a service.

commitment An agreement between a lender and a borrower to loan money at a future date, provided specified conditions are met.

commitment fee The payment made by a potential borrower to a potential lender for the lender's promise to lend money at a specified future date.

commitment letter A letter from the lender to the borrower stating that the loan application has been approved for a specific amount, term and rate and listing the conditions under which the loan funds will be disbursed.

commodities futures The contracts for future delivery of economic goods, such as agricultural and mining products or securities, at a predetermined price; these contracts are traded on commodities exchanges. *See also* financial futures.

common law The body of law developed in England primarily from judicial decisions based on custom and precedent, unwritten in statute or code, and constituting the basis of the English legal system and of the system in all of the United States except Louisiana.

common stock The shares of a corporation, representing proportionate ownership or equity, that give the holder an unlimited interest in the corporation's earnings and assets after prior claims have been met. *See also* stock.

community property   A form of joint ownership by husband and wife, recognized in certain states, which considers each spouse to have a one-half ownership interest in the property, regardless of his or her individual contribution. Community property includes all property that was (1) gained or earned by either spouse during marriage, (2) not owned individually at the time of marriage, and (3) not acquired by either spouse during marriage by inheritance, will or gift.

Community Reinvestment Act of 1977 (CRA)   The federal legislation that requires financial institutions to delineate their communities and to explain how they serve their communities' credit needs. Institutions must, among other procedures, prepare a CRA statement, display a CRA notice and maintain a public comment file.

compensating balance   The demand deposit or other noninterest-bearing deposit made to a financial institution by a business to obtain credit.

compound interest   The interest that accrues when earnings for a specified period are added to principal, so that interest for the following period is computed on the principal plus accumulated interest.

condemnation   The legal process for taking private property for public use, under the right of eminent domain, with just compensation to the owner.

conditional endorsement   A type of restrictive endorsement on a negotiable instrument that designates both the next titleholder and conditions to the endorser's liability.

condominium   A system of direct ownership of a single unit in a multiunit structure. The individual holds legal title to his or her unit and owns the common areas of the structure and the land jointly with other owners. The owners may sell their unit to anyone; the owners pay individual property taxes and may claim tax exemptions just as they would if they owned a free standing single-family home.

conduit   1. A type of rollover IRA for use by individuals who want to roll over all or any portion of a lump-sum distribution from one retirement plan to another. 2. A firm that issues mortgage-backed securities based on mortgage loans it purchases from a number of lenders.

conforming mortgage loan   A mortgage loan that conforms to regulatory limits such as loan-to-value ratio, term and other characteristics.

conservator   A court-appointed fiduciary, or guardian, who handles an individual's or entity's funds. A conservator for an individual is usually appointed when that individual is legally declared incapable of managing his or her own affairs because of mental incompetence or physical disability. A conservator for an entity is appointed to preserve the assets of the business. The FDIC and the RTC may act as a conservator of any federally insured depository institution.

consolidated metropolitan statistical area (CMSA) A geographic unit composed of two or more adjacent standard metropolitan statistical areas having a combined population of 1 million or more, with close social and economic links. Formerly known as standard consolidated statistical areas.

construction loan A short-term loan for financing the cost of construction. The lender makes payouts to the builder at periodic intervals as the work progresses.

construction loan agreement A written agreement between a lender and a builder or borrower with respect to a construction loan. The agreement defines the amount of funds for construction, describes permitted uses of the funds and the payout procedure, and provides for completion of construction in accordance with approved plans and specifications.

consumer bank *See* nonbank bank.

consumer credit The credit extended to a natural person for personal, family or household purposes.

Consumer Credit Protection Act *See* Truth-in-Lending Act.

consumer loan A secured or unsecured loan to a natural person for personal, family or household purposes; consumer credit can be open- or closed-end credit.

consumer price index (CPI) A statistical device calculated by the Bureau of Labor Statistics, U.S. Department of Labor. The index is used to measure changes in the cost of living for consumers.

consummation A term, defined under Regulation Z, meaning the actual time that a contractual relationship is created between borrower and lender, irrespective of the time of performance of a particular transaction. Depending upon the state law of contracts governing a particular institution, consummation may occur at the time a loan is closed, at the time a lender accepts (as distinct from receives) a borrower's loan application or at the time a firm commitment is given to make a loan.

continuous compounding A term that refers to compounding over the smallest time interval possible and that yields the highest effective interest rate.

contract A binding agreement between two or more persons or parties.

contract for deed A written agreement between the seller and buyer of a piece of property, whereby the buyer receives title to the property only after making a determined number of monthly payments; also called an installment contract or land contract.

C

contributory IRA   A type of Individual Retirement Account established by individuals who set aside all or a portion of their yearly compensation; also called a regular or individual IRA.

controller   A chief financial operations officer of an institution. The controller is responsible for supervising the operations of the accounting department and preparing its financial reports, reporting to management and evaluating the financial position of the institution for management.

conventional loan   A mortgage loan made by a savings institution without FHA insurance or VA guarantee; called a conventional loan because it conforms to accepted standards, modified within legal bounds by mutual consent of the borrower and the lender.

conversion   A term in the financial service business that refers to a change of ownership from mutual to stock (or vice versa) or a change of charter from state to federal (or vice versa).

conversion clause   A provision, in some adjustable rate loans, that allows the borrower to change from an adjustable to a fixed-rate loan at a specified time during the term of the loan.

convertible   The term used for a bond or preferred stock that, under specified conditions, may be exchanged for common stock or another security, usually of the same corporation.

cooperative   A system of indirect ownership of a single unit in a multiunit structure. The individual owns shares in a nonprofit corporation that holds title to the building; the corporation, in turn, gives the owner a long-term proprietary lease on the unit.

co-operative bank   The legal name used in Massachusetts, and sometimes in New Hampshire, Rhode Island and Vermont, for a state-chartered savings association.

corporation   A form of business organization legally binding a group of individuals to act as one entity, carrying on one or more related enterprises and having the powers, rights and privileges of an individual; the corporation continues to exist regardless of changes in its membership or ownership.

correspondent bank   A financial institution that provides one or more services for another institution in return for the maintenance of deposit balances and/or fees. Typical services are check handling for out-of-area checks, trust services and technical services.

cosigner   An individual or entity that signs a legal document on an equal basis with the signer. On a promissory note, all cosigners are individually and jointly liable for repayment of the full debt.

cost accounting   The process of collecting and summarizing the operational revenue and expense items of a firm and analyzing their behavior to facilitate internal decision making and performance appraisal.

cost approach to value   An approximation of the market value of improved real estate measured as reproduction cost or replacement cost.

cost of funds   The average amount, typically expressed as an interest rate percentage, that a depository institution pays on all of its deposits and borrowings. An institution will subtract its cost of funds from its total investment portfolio yield (which typically includes mortgages and consumer loans) to determine its spread. *See also* portfolio yield; rate of return; yield.

cost of living   The amount of money necessary to pay taxes and to purchase goods and services related to a given standard of living. Unlike the consumer price index, the cost of living takes into account changes in buying patterns and tastes.

countersignature   An additional signature given to attest the authenticity of an instrument.

coupon bond   A debt obligation on which the bondholder collects interest regularly by clipping attached coupons as they mature and presenting them for payment to the bond issuer. Beginning in 1983, no bonds issued with maturities of more than one year will come in bearer form. *See also* registered bond.

coupon book   A set of payment cards or computer cards that the borrower returns to the institution one at a time with regular loan repayments or with deposits for savings accounts such as a club account.

covenant   A constraint in a loan agreement that sets forth certain requirements as to what the borrower will and will not do.

CPA   *See* certified public accountant.

CPI   *See* consumer price index.

CRA   *See* Community Reinvestment Act of 1977.

creative financing   A type of financing other than traditional fixed-rate, fixed-term financing.

credit   **1.** The exchange of goods or services on the promise of future payment. *See also* consumer credit. **2.** An accounting term that refers to the right-hand side of an account record in which the amounts are entered in a double-entry system of bookkeeping.

credit analysis   A determination of the risk inherent in making a loan or extending credit to a particular person or business, including consideration of the loan applicant's income, expenses, past use of credit and general ability to manage financial affairs.

credit bureau   An agency that collects and distributes credit-history information on individuals and businesses.

credit card   A plastic card that can be used by the cardholder to make purchases or obtain cash advances utilizing a line of credit made available to the cardholder by the card-issuing financial institution.

credit life insurance   A type of insurance on the life of a borrower that pays off a specified debt if the borrower dies.

credit rating   A professional estimate of the financial position and integrity of a person or company, based on present financial condition, past credit history and other relevant factors.

credit risk   The degree of loan repayment uncertainty or risk that the institution assumes in advancing funds to a borrower; it is based upon credit information obtained.

credit union   A cooperative organization chartered by a state government or the federal government for the purpose of collecting deposits from members and making loans to members at a low interest rate.

creditor   An individual or business to whom money or something of value is owed.

cross-selling   The process of offering additional services to a customer who already is using one or more services; e.g., explaining the advantages of a telephone transfer account to a customer making a deposit to a regular savings account.

cumulative dividends   A feature of preferred stock that requires all preferred dividends in arrears (dividends not paid to stockholders for previous periods) to be paid before any common dividends are paid.

cumulative voting plan   A management policy of a stock corporation wherein the total number of votes a stockholder can exercise is determined by multiplying the number of shares owned by the number of directors to be elected.

currency   Coins or paper money used as a medium of exchange.

currency transaction report   The Internal Revenue Service Form 4789 completed by financial institutions, as required by the Bank Secrecy Act, to report large or suspicious cash transactions to the Treasury Department. *See also* Bank Secrecy Act.

current asset   An asset expected to be converted into cash within 12 months.

current liability   A liability scheduled to be paid within the next 12 months.

current ratio   An indicator used in analyzing a firm's liquidity position; it is computed by dividing current assets by current liabilities.

current yield   The annual income divided by the current price of the security; annual return.

custodial gift   A gift to a minor child from an adult who retains control over the gift, or grants such control to another adult, until the child reaches majority and legally can accept responsibility for the gift.

custodial IRA   An IRA in which a fiduciary relationship is created. Laws and regulations on Individual Retirement Accounts view most custodians as having all of the powers and responsibilities of a trustee. Under state law, there may be some technical legal distinctions relating to the powers of custodians as compared to trustees, but this is a matter for legal experts. Federal law does not distinguish between custodial and trusteed IRAs. *See also* trust.

D

D and O insurance The insurance that protects directors and officers of financial institutions from liability due to errors and omissions committed while acting on behalf of the institution.

dealer A person or business entity that acts as a middleman to facilitate the distribution of consumer goods from the manufacturer to the public. The dealer buys merchandise from the manufacturer and sells it to the consumer for a profit.

dealer paper The retail installment contracts purchased by a financial institution for a price negotiated with a dealer. The transfer of the contract from dealer to institution is evidenced by execution of the assignment section of the contract.

dealer reserve The portion of dealer income held by the institution as protection against the possibility that dealers might default on their obligations as spelled out in the dealer's agreement.

debenture An unsecured corporate bond that is backed only by the general credit and strength of the issuing corporation.

debit A charge to a customer's access account or a charge against a customer's deposit account. Also, in accounting, a debit refers to an entry on the left-hand side of an account record in which amounts are recorded in a double-entry system of bookkeeping.

debit card A plastic card designed to give a customer access to funds in his or her deposit account to obtain cash or effect a transfer of funds.

debt to income ratio The ratio that expresses the relationship of the sum of the applicant's monthly credit obligations to his or her monthly income.

debtor A person who owes money or something else of value.

decedent A deceased person, ordinarily used with respect to one who has died recently. A deposit account held in the name of an executor or administrator of a deceased person's estate is called a decedent estate account.

declaration of condominium ownership A complex legal document, with appropriate addenda, that provides for qualifying a multiunit property for condominium development and sale in accordance with a state's condominium act (law).

declining balance depreciation method A systematic conversion of an asset's cost into a periodic expense whereby a fixed percentage rate is applied to the decreasing book value of the asset.

deed   A written agreement in proper legal form that transfers ownership of land from one party to another. *See also* quit claim deed; warranty deed.

deed absolute   *See* deed given to secure a debt.

deed given to secure a debt   A form of mortgage in which title to the property is handed over to the lender by the borrower as security for the repayment of a debt; also called a deed absolute.

deed in lieu of foreclosure   A transfer of title to real property from a delinquent mortgagor to the mortgagee, given to satisfy the balance due on the defaulted loan.

deed of trust   A legal document, used in some states, that conveys title to real estate to a disinterested third party, who holds title until the owner of the property has repaid the debt; accomplishes essentially the same purpose as a regular mortgage. *See also* trust indenture.

default   The failure to do what is required by law or by the terms of a contract.

deferred expense   An expense paid for in one accounting period but whose recognition is delayed to subsequent accounting periods, such as a prepaid insurance premium.

deferred income   The income received during one accounting period but earned in a subsequent period or periods, such as advance collection of interest on a loan.

deficiency judgment   A legal judgment given when the property securing a debt is insufficient to satisfy the remaining debt.

deflation   An economic condition in which the purchasing power of the dollar increases; a reduction in the general level of prices. *See also* inflation.

delinquency rates   The percentage of overdue loans in relation to the total amount of loans outstanding.

demand deposit   An account that is withdrawable by check at the demand of the depositor; also called a checking account. Demand deposits are noninterest bearing and are subject to federal reserve requirements. *See also* Regulation D.

denomination   The value or size of a series of coins or paper money.

de novo institution   A new institution.

Department of Housing and Urban Development (HUD)   The cabinet department of the federal government responsible for federal housing programs and urban affairs; it governs FHA and GNMA operations.

D

deposit   The placement of funds in an account at a financial institution subject to terms agreed upon by the depositor and the institution.

deposit account   The funds placed in an account that can be withdrawn only by the owner(s) or a duly authorized agent, or on the owner's nontransferable order; sometimes called a savings deposit or share account. *See also* individual entries, such as certificate account; individual account; joint tenancy account; etc.

deposit account contract   The contractual relationship encompassing all of the terms and conditions to which the customer and the savings institution are subject when the customer opens a deposit account; usually contained, in part, in the signature card.

Depository Institutions Act of 1982   A federal law, also known as the Garn-St Germain Act, that touched on a range of activities for commercial banks, thrifts and credit unions. Major provisions include expanded lending powers for depository institutions, new investment authorities, noncash capital assistance for qualified financial institutions, and a requirement that federal financial regulators develop a "money market" account for banks and thrifts.

Depository Institutions Deregulation and Monetary Control Act of 1980   A federal law affecting all depository institutions. Among the important provisions of the law were an orderly phaseout of regulated maximum interest rates on accounts in depository institutions; an increase on federal insurance for individually owned deposit accounts; and nationwide authorization of NOW accounts. The law expanded the influence of the Federal Reserve System on all financial institutions by changing reserve requirements on certain accounts and expanding access to certain Federal Reserve Services to all depository institutions. Provisions specifically affecting federal savings institutions included increased authorization to make consumer loans and authorization to engage in credit card operations.

depreciation   The decline in the dollar value of an asset over time and through use. For tax purposes, the dollar amount of annual depreciation may be computed differently from the actual decline in value.

development loan   A loan made for the purpose of preparing raw land for the construction of buildings. Preparation may include grading and installation of utilities and roadways.

direct deposit   A preauthorized payment system in which customers' government benefits, payroll checks, interest or dividend checks, pension, or any other regularly received credits are automatically deposited to their checking or deposit accounts.

Director of the Office of Thrift Supervision (DOTS) An individual authorized to supervise the examination and regulation of savings associations and to prescribe uniform accounting and disclosure standards. The OTS director is appointed by the president, with Senate confirmation, to serve a five-year term. The director also serves as one of five members of the FDIC board. *See also* OTS.

direct reduction The application of loan repayments directly to loan principal. *See also* amortization.

direct transfer The moving of IRA funds from one IRA trustee directly to another IRA trustee, with no check made payable to the IRA participant. The direct transfer is not subject to any time or frequency restrictions.

disclosure statements The information required by government regulations to be given to a borrower prior to consummation of a loan.

discount The difference between the selling price and the par (face) value of a bond. A bond selling at a discount sells for less than its par value.

discount broker A stockbroker or brokerage house that processes the purchase or sale of securities at a discount from the customary broker commission. Generally, the discount broker does not provide market advice.

discount certificates The certificates of deposit offered at an issue price that is less than the stated maturity value. The difference between the issue price (amount invested) and the stated redemption value of the account at maturity is called the original issue discount. Savings institutions can offer discount certificates on any time deposit that the institution offers.

discount interest A type of interest that is determined by calculating the total amount of interest for the loan and subtracting it from the principal loan amount. The borrower receives the net loan amount (the difference between the principal loan amount and interest amount) but agrees to repay the principal loan amount.

discount rate The interest rate charged by the Federal Reserve Banks on loans to their member banks.

discounted interest A deduction from principal for finance charges at the time a loan is made. The remaining amount is repaid through installment payments.

discounted price The price of a security (usually a bond) that sells at less than its face value. The security accrues interest until it reaches its face value at maturity.

discounting   The advance deduction of interest from the principal amount of a loan, so that the borrower receives the principal amount less the interest due over the term of the loan, but repays the full principal amount; suitable only for short-term loans.

disintermediation   The process by which individuals build up their holdings of market instruments, such as U.S. government and agency issues, stocks and bonds, and slow down additions to their deposit accounts at financial institutions. *See also* financial intermediary.

dividend   The portion of a corporation's profits paid to each stockholder as a return on the stockholder's investment.

doing business statutes   The state laws that define the licensing and other conditions under which a corporation, or other entity licensed by another state or the federal government, may conduct business in a state.

domicile   The place where a person has his or her true, fixed, permanent home and principal establishment and to which, whenever he or she is absent, he or she has the intention of returning. The term is not synonymous with residence; a person may have several residences but only one domicile.

dormant account   A deposit account on which no transaction (except the crediting of earnings) has occurred for a specified number of years. At the end of the specified time period, funds in the account escheat to the state.

DOTS   *See* Director of the Office of Thrift Supervision.

double entry   A method of bookkeeping in which there are two entries for each transaction, one as a debit and the other as a credit. The entries check and balance each other.

draft   An order for the payment of money, drawn by one person or organization on another; a bill of exchange payable on demand. *See also* bank draft; sight draft.

draw   The release of a portion of the construction loan proceeds according to the schedule of payments in the loan agreement; also called advance, disbursement, payout or take down.

drawee   The bank on which a check is drawn.

drawer   The party who issues an order, draft, check or bill of exchange.

due-on-sale clause   A mortgage clause that demands payment of the entire loan balance upon sale or other transfer of the real estate securing the loan.

25

E

earnest money   A cash deposit that a home buyer must supply as evidence of his or her good-faith intention to complete the transaction. The deposit represents a percentage of the accepted selling price and is given to a third party to be held in an escrow account. The earnest money may be forfeited to the seller if the buyer does not comply with the purchase agreement.

earnings   *See* interest.

earnings per share (EPS)   The total after-tax earnings of a corporation divided by the total number of its shares outstanding.

easement   An interest in land granted by the landowner for the benefit of another, entitling its holder to specific limited uses or privileges, such as the right to construct and maintain a roadway across the property or the right to construct pipelines under or powerlines over the land. Party wall easements, which share a common foundation, are commonplace in town house and condominium apartments.

ECOA   *See* Equal Credit Opportunity Act.

economic life   The length of time over which a piece of property may be put to profitable use. Usually, less than the physical life.

economic obsolescence   The loss of property value caused by environmental factors outside the property itself, such as a change in zoning laws.

economic rent   The amount of rental a property likely would command in the open market if it were vacant and available for rent.

education loan   An advance of funds made to a student for the financing of a college or vocational education. Various programs are funded through federal or state agencies or private organizations.

effective interest rate   The actual return one receives on an investment. *See also* effective yield.

effective yield   The actual rate of return to the investor. *See also* effective interest rate.

EFTS   *See* electronic funds transfer system.

electronic funds transfer system (EFTS)   A system whereby financial information is transferred from the deposit account of the payer to the deposit account of the payee. The payment message may be executed instantaneously, as in a purchase transaction at the retail point-of-sale terminal, or it may be executed on a batch basis, as in the daily distribution of transactions by the automated clearinghouse to member financial institutions.

eminent domain   The right of a government to obtain ownership of private property for public use such as a street or park; compensation is made to the owner.

Employees Retirement Income Security Act of 1974 (ERISA)   A federal law that established minimum federal levels of acceptability for private pension plans.

encumbrance   A claim or liability attached to real property, such as a mortgage or unpaid taxes. *See also* lien.

endorsee   The person or entity to whom a bill of exchange, promissory note, check or other negotiable instrument is endorsed.

endorsement   A signature written by hand or stamped on the back of a negotiable instrument whereby the ownership thereof is assigned or transferred to another. *See also* blank endorsement; restrictive endorsement; special endorsement.

endorser   The person or entity that endorses a negotiable instrument.

EPS   *See* earnings per share.

Equal Credit Opportunity Act (ECOA)   A federal law that makes it illegal for creditors to discriminate against any applicant on the basis of sex, marital status, race, color, religion, national origin, receipt of public assistance benefits or the borrower's good faith exercise of rights under the Consumer Credit Protection Act. *See also* Regulation B.

equitable right of redemption   A privilege granted by states to borrowers allowing a certain amount of time before the foreclosure sale during which borrowers can pay the outstanding loan balance and recover the property. *See also* redemption period; statutory right of redemption.

equity   The owner's interest in a property. In its simplest form it may be expressed: Equity = Assets − Liabilities.

equity line of credit   An open-end loan that is secured by the borrower's ownership interest in real property and that may be made for a variety of purposes. *See also* line of credit.

equity loan   A loan that uses the borrower's equity in real property as security. An equity loan, which may be made for a variety of purposes, is also known as a second or junior mortgage loan.

ERISA   *See* Employee Retirement Income Security Act of 1974.

errors and omissions insurance   A form of insurance coverage that protects the financial institution against liability in the event that it fails to procure or maintain agreed-upon insurance coverage for a borrower.

escalator clause   A provision for rental increases during the term of the lease based on an index beyond the control of the lessor or lessee.

escheat   The reversion of property ownership to the state if the owner dies intestate and without heirs.

escrow   A written agreement among three or more persons, under which documents or property being transferred from one person to another is placed with the third person as custodian; the transfer is completed only upon the fulfillment of certain specified conditions.

escrow account   An account held by the financial institution in which a borrower pays monthly installment payments for property taxes, insurance and special assessments, and from which the lender disburses these sums as they become due. Also called reserve, impoundment or trust account.

escrow closing   A kind of loan closing in which an escrow agent (a disinterested third party) accepts the loan funds and mortgage from the lender, the downpayment from the buyer and the deed from the seller.

estate   The ownership rights that a person has to lands or other property; the term also denotes the property itself. *See also* leasehold estate.

estate planning   The orderly process of planning assets, bequests and estate disposition for such purposes as insuring liquidity, providing for family needs, and avoiding forced sales and unnecessary taxes.

examiner   An individual engaged by the federal or state supervisory authorities to examine the operations of the savings institutions within their jurisdiction.

exception   An item that may not be covered by title insurance because it limits in some way the owner's rights to his or her property; exceptions may include easements, liens and deed restrictions.

exception items   The checks or negotiable orders of withdrawal, received by the drawee institution, that cannot be paid for one reason or another.

excess contribution   An amount greater than the Individual Retirement Account participant's annual allowable contribution. An excess contribution is subject to a 6% penalty imposed on the participant by the Internal Revenue Service. *See also* allowable contributions.

exculpatory clause   A clause in a trust instrument relieving the trustee of liability for any act performed in good faith under the trust instrument.

executor/executrix   The individual appointed in a will and approved by a probate court to administer the disposition of an estate according to directions in the will.

expenses   The disbursements of the firm; the cost of goods sold or services rendered during a given time period.

F

face value   The value of a bond at which it can be redeemed at maturity. Same as its "redemption value." Face value also is called *par value* in bonds; the term should not be confused with the par value of stocks.

factoring   A financing method used in commercial lending whereby the firm sells its accounts receivable to a financial institution.

Fair Credit Billing Act   The federal legislation, enacted and made part of the Consumer Protection Act in 1974, that is designed to provide consumers with the opportunity to question amounts billed to them by creditors. The debtor can question the accuracy of the billing statement by writing to the creditor within 60 days of receiving the statement. Between the time that the auditor receives the letter from the debtor and responds accordingly, the debtor is not required to submit payment for the disputed amount.

Fair Credit Reporting Act   The 1971 federal law designed to protect consumers from inaccurate credit information. The Act lists the rights of consumers with regard to both credit grantors and consumer-credit reporting agencies.

Fair Debt Collection Practices Act   A part of the federal Consumer Credit Protection Act, effective in 1978, designed to cover primarily independent debt collectors and third parties who collect debts for others, and to protect consumers from a variety of unfair, abusive and deceptive debt collection practices.

fair lending practices regulations   The federal regulations that pertain to the application and appraisal practices of federal institutions. The regulations prohibit the use of discriminatory appraisals and require the preparation of written loan underwriting standards, the collection of monitoring information and the maintenance of loan application registers. *See also* loan underwriting standards.

Fannie Mae   *See* Federal National Mortgage Association.

Farmers Home Administration (FmHA)   An agency of the federal government that makes, participates in and insures loans for the construction and purchase of homes in rural communities.

FASB   *See* Financial Accounting Standards Board.

FDIC   *See* Federal Deposit Insurance Corporation.

Federal Deposit Insurance Corporation (FDIC)   An instrumentality of the federal government that insures the deposits of member depository institutions, including commercial banks, savings associations and savings banks. The FDIC administers two subfunds, the Bank Insurance Fund (BIF) and the Savings Association Insurance Fund (SAIF), and is responsible for the supervision, examination and regulation of insured institutions under its authority. The five-member FDIC board includes the Comptroller of the Currency, the Director of the Office of Thrift Supervision and three presidential appointees. *See also* BIF; SAIF; OCC; DOTS.

Federal funds interest rate   The interest rate charged on overnight loans between banks. These funds are immediately available from reserve accounts at Federal Reserve banks and are commonly called Fed funds. Fed funds are borrowed ("bought") or loaned ("sold") for purposes of meeting the Federal Reserve's legal reserve requirement. *See also* Regulation D.

Federal Home Loan Bank   One of the 12 regional banks of the Federal Home Loan Bank System that provides credit to member savings institutions, savings banks, life insurance companies and other qualifying institutions.

Federal Home Loan Bank System   A federally established system made up of the Federal Housing Finance Board (FHFB); the 12 regional Federal Home Loan Banks; and member savings associations, savings banks, life insurance companies and other qualifying institutions. The fundamental purpose of the system is to serve as a central credit facility for member institutions.

Federal Home Loan Mortgage Corporation (FHLMC)   A secondary market facility of the Federal Home Loan Bank System that buys and sells conventional, FHA and VA loans, and participating interests in blocks of such loans; commonly called the Mortgage Corporation or Freddie Mac.

Federal Housing Administration (FHA)   A government agency within the Department of Housing and Urban Development that administers many programs for housing loans made under its auspices with private funds, including mortgage insurance for lenders and rent or interest assistance for low-income tenants and mortgagors.

Federal Housing Finance Board (FHFB)   The federal body created by Title VII of FIRREA that succeeds the Federal Home Loan Bank Board as overseer and supervisor of the FHLBanks. The FHFB may officially announce and enforce regulations to ensure that the FHLBanks carry out their housing finance mission, operate in a safe and sound manner, and remain adequately capitalized and capable of raising funds in the capital markets. *See also* FIRREA.

Federal Insurance Contribution Act (FICA)   A federal act that combined Social Security, old age, survivors, disability and hospital insurance tax into a single tax. Details and coverage are changed frequently by Congress.

Federal National Mortgage Association (FNMA) A government-sponsored but privately owned secondary mortgage market corporation that buys and sells mortgage-backed securities and FHA, VA and conventional loans; commonly called Fannie Mae.

federal reserve note The paper currency placed in circulation by the Federal Reserve Banks and issued in denominations ranging from $1 to $100.

F

Federal Reserve System The group made up of the Federal Reserve Board, the 12 district Federal Reserve Banks and nationally chartered commercial banks. The Federal Reserve System serves as a credit facility for member commercial banks and controls the nation's money supply by regulating its requirements on reserves.

federal savings institution A specialized financial institution chartered and regulated by the Office of Thrift Supervision (OTS). *See also* OTS.

fee simple estate A type of real estate ownership in which the owner is entitled to all of the rights and privileges, and accountable for the responsibilities, incident to his or her property.

FHA *See* Federal Housing Administration.

FHA Title I loan A loan for the purpose of home improvement. It is insured for 90% of loss by the Federal Housing Administration if the borrower does not repay.

FHFB *See* Federal Housing Finance Board.

FHLMC *See* Federal Home Loan Mortgage Corporation.

FICA *See* Federal Insurance Contribution Act.

fiduciary A person or corporation with the responsibility of holding or controlling property for another.

fiduciary account A deposit account containing funds owned by one individual but administered for that individual's benefit by another individual who is legally appointed as conservator, trustee, agent or other fiduciary.

FIFO An acronym for first in, first out. In savings terminology, a method of determining deposit account earnings. Earnings are computed on the balance of the deposit account at the beginning of the earnings period, plus additions received during the period, minus withdrawals that are charged against the earliest amount in the account. In accounting, a system of inventory evaluations. *See also* LIFO.

finance charges The sum of all charges payable directly or indirectly by the borrower and imposed directly by the creditor as an incident or condition of the extension of credit. Finance charges must be included on truth-in-lending disclosures and described as the total dollar amount the consumer pays for the use of credit.

Financial Accounting Standards Board (FASB) An independent, seven-member board that is influential in the development of accounting standards in the private sector.

financial futures The contracts based on financial instruments (treasury securities, certificates of deposit and others) whose prices fluctuate with changes in interest rates. Financial futures represent a firm commitment to buy or sell a specific financial instrument at a specified time and at a price established in a central, regulated marketplace. *See also* commodities futures.

financial institution A corporation chartered for the purpose of dealing primarily with money, such as deposits, investments and loans, rather than in goods or other services.

Financial Institutions Reform, Recovery and Enforcement Act of 1989 (FIRREA) A federal law consisting of 14 titles, most of which directly or indirectly affect savings associations. The major purposes of the act were to reform, recapitalize and consolidate the federal deposit insurance system, and to enhance the regulatory and enforcement powers of federal financial institution regulatory agencies. *See also* FHFB; OTS; RTC; FDIC; BIF; SAIF; and Qualified Thrift Lender Test.

financial intermediary A financial institution that accepts money from savers and investors and uses those funds to make loans and other investments in its own name; includes savings associations, mutual savings banks, commercial banks, life insurance companies, credit unions and investment companies. *See also* disintermediation; intermediation.

financial leverage The use of borrowed funds in an effort to increase the return on equity. *See also* operating leverage.

financial ratios The measures of the operating results and financial condition of a business that relate one item on the balance sheet (or income statement) with another. Financial ratios are used to assess a firm's past and present condition.

financial statements The reports that represent a summary of a firm's accounting data and reflect the firm's financial condition. The four basic financial statements are the balance sheet, income statement, statement of retained earnings and statement of changes in financial position.

financing statement A document, filed at a designated public office, that serves as public notice to third parties that a lender has established security interest in collateral.

FIRREA *See* Financial Institutions Reform, Recovery and Enforcement Act of 1989.

fiscal policy The federal government taxation and financial activities, largely in the hands of the President and Congress. *See also* monetary policy.

fixed annuity   The guaranteed income, received at regular intervals, for which the basic amount of each payment has been fixed in advance; minor variations may occur with interest rate changes.

fixed assets   The tangible assets, such as office buildings, furniture, fixtures and equipment, that are used in the operation of a business, that have a relatively long life and that are not intended to be sold in the normal process of the business.

F

fixed income investment   A type of investment in which the dividend, interest or rental income is fixed contractually.

fixed-rate mortgage   The term commonly used to describe a mortgage loan with a constant interest rate and payment throughout the life of the loan. The periodic payments of principal and interest made by the borrower during the term of the loan result in the mortgage loan being paid in full at maturity.

flexible payment mortgage (FPM)   An alternative mortgage loan program in which the borrower pays only interest on the loan for up to five years. After this period, payments are increased to include principal and interest to amortize the loan over the remaining term.

float   The time that elapses between the day a check is issued and the day it is presented to the drawee institution for the funds to be transferred.

floor plan   An architectural drawing of the length and width of a building and the arrangement of rooms illustrated in a horizontal section taken at some distance above the floor. The plan shows walls, windows, doors and other architectural features. Mechanical floor plans show heating, cooling and plumbing equipment and lines; electrical floor plans show lighting fixtures, electrical equipment and convenience outlets, as well as switches and sometimes circuits.

floor planning   The loans made to finance dealers' inventory purchases.

flowchart   A diagram showing a logical sequence of operations or actions. Symbols and interconnecting lines are used to represent the function to be performed and to indicate when it is to be performed.

FmHA   *See* Farmers Home Administration.

FNMA   *See* Federal National Mortgage Association.

forbearance   The act by the lender of refraining from taking legal action on a mortgage that is delinquent, usually contingent upon the borrower's performing certain agreed-upon actions.

foreclosure   The legal action that bars a defaulted mortgagor's right to redeem the mortgaged property. This action is brought about to satisfy the outstanding balance on a mortgage loan; usually, it results in the secured property being sold at public auction.

foreclosure by court action   A legal procedure in which the lender files suit against the defaulting borrower, and the court issues a decree establishing a debt and arranges for public sale of the property by a court officer.

foreclosure under power of sale   A legal procedure, permissible in some states, in which the institution exercises a right, expressed in the loan documents, to take over the property of the defaulting borrower without court action and offer it at public sale to the highest bidder.

forgery   The false making or altering of any written instrument with intent to defraud.

forward commitment contract   An agreement between buyers and sellers of loans to purchase or sell loans at a specified future date according to terms outlined in the agreement.

401K   A tax-deferred savings plan that allows employees to contribute up to a specified percentage of their salaries into one or more employer-selected plans. Employee contributions are made with pretax dollars, which are not reported for income-tax purposes. Employers usually match employee contributions in a specified way. Also called a salary reduction plan.

FPM   *See* flexible payment mortgage.

Freddie Mac   *See* Federal Home Loan Mortgage Corporation.

full faith and credit bond   *See* general obligation bond.

fully amortizing loan   A loan in which the principal and interest will be repaid fully through regular installments by the time the loan matures.

future advances clause   A clause in a mortgage instrument that allows a lender to advance additional funds without executing a new mortgage instrument.

future value   The amount to which a sum of money earning compound interest will grow by a certain date.

futures contract   A binding agreement that specifies that on a certain date and at a certain place, a minimum grade of a standardized quantity of commodities or securities is to be delivered and paid for in full; contracts are traded only on the exchange which issued them.

futures exchange   A membership organization, like the stock exchange, that provides a place where its members can trade commodities or securities for future delivery in a controlled, orderly manner.

futures market   The market in which futures contracts are bought and sold on many basic fibers, foodstuffs, metals, currencies and financial instruments.

G

GAAP   *See* generally accepted accounting principles.

gap management   The attempt to bring the dollar difference between rate-sensitive assets and rate-sensitive liabilities to zero or as close to zero as possible.

Garn-St Germain Act   *See* Depository Institutions Act of 1982.

general ledger   A record or legend that shows increases and decreases for each asset, liability, reserve, capital, income and expense account. Each individual account is called a general ledger account.

general obligation bond   A bond formally sanctioned by either the voting public or its legislature. The governmental promise to repay the principal and pay interest is constitutionally guaranteed by virtue of the government's right to tax the population. *See also* revenue bond.

general reserves   The funds set aside for the sole purpose of covering possible losses. Includes the Federal Insurance Reserve, Reserve for Contingencies and any reserve "locked up" for losses.

generally accepted accounting principles (GAAP)   The accounting theory and procedures adopted by the accounting profession to facilitate uniformity and understanding in preparing financial statements.

Ginnie Mae   *See* Government National Mortgage Association.

Glass-Steagall Act   *See* Banking Act of 1933.

GNP   *See* gross national product.

good faith estimate   A disclosure required under the Real Estate Settlement Procedures Act (RESPA) that must be given to all mortgage loan applicants at application time. The disclosure is an estimate of all settlement charges likely to be incurred at closing.

goodwill   An intangible asset derived from a business' favorable reputation, advantageous location or other characteristic. *See also* intangible asset.

Government National Mortgage Association (GNMA)   A government corporation, supervised by the Department of Housing and Urban Development, that provides special assistance for the purchase of certain FHA and VA mortgages and guarantees securities backed by pools of mortgage loans; commonly called Ginnie Mae.

grace period   A specified period after the regular due date of a loan payment during which no collection procedures are begun and no late charge or other penalty is assessed. Payments submitted within the grace period generally do not adversely affect the borrower's permanent credit history.

grace period provision   A clause in a promissory note stating that a borrower who has prepaid a loan may at any time skip payments until the loan balance equals the amount it would have been if the borrower had not prepaid.

grantor   The person who makes a settlement or creates a trust of property; also called a settlor.

gross income   All income that is not legally exempt from tax.

gross national product (GNP)   The total market value of all goods and services produced by a nation in a specified period of time.

gross operating income   An accounting term that includes income received from the ordinary operation of the business before deducting expenses of operation.

guarantor   The individual or entity that guarantees to repay a debt if the borrower defaults.

H

hazard insurance   A form of insurance coverage for real estate that includes protection against loss from fire, certain natural causes, vandalism and malicious mischief.

hedge   A way to protect oneself against a possible investment loss by making a counterbalancing transaction.

highest and best use   An appraisal concept that considers all the possible, permissible and profitable uses of a property site to estimate the use that will provide the owner with the highest net return on the investment, consistent with the existing neighboring land uses.

hold   A notation made on an account record to show that a specific amount of money temporarily is withheld from the available balance. A hold may be placed on a checking account or regular deposit account to show a certain amount is not available to the owner or to show that the account requires special handling.

holder-in-due-course rule   **1.** A rule, contained in the Uniform Commercial Code, which originally stated that subsequent purchases of a promissory note are not subject to any claims regarding the initial transaction. This rule was amended in 1976 by the Federal Trade Commission to require all subsequent holders of a note to be subject to claims against the seller. **2.** A rule, contained in the Uniform Commercial Code, that pertains to NOW draft and check negotiability. If a check or NOW draft is negotiated to a third party who has no particular knowledge of the prior transaction, that third party takes the check or NOW draft free and clear of any defenses existing between the original parties—drawer (e.g., consumer) and payee (e.g., merchant). The innocent third party has a right to receive payment for the check, even though the drawer is dissatisfied with the payee's merchandise.

holding company   A corporation that owns stock of another corporation and, in most cases, has a voting control over that corporation.

home   A residential structure containing one, two, three or four dwelling units, as defined in government statistics.

home equity loan   *See* junior lien.

home financing   The providing of funds, secured by a mortgage, for the purchase or construction or improvement of a residential structure containing one, two, three or four dwelling units.

home improvement loan   An advance of funds, usually not secured by a mortgage and usually short-term, made to a property owner for the upgrading of residential property, such as maintenance and repair, additions and alterations or replacement of equipment or structural elements.

Home Mortgage Disclosure Act   The federal law enacted in 1975 requiring the disclosure of mortgage loan data by depository institutions that are located in metropolitan statistical areas and that make federally related mortgage loans. Those institutions subject to the Act are required to disclose to the public aggregate mortgage loan data in terms of number of loans and total dollar amounts with respect to all mortgage loans that they originate and purchase each year.

homeowner's insurance   A broad form of real estate insurance coverage that combines hazard insurance with personal liability protection and other items.

Home Owners' Loan Act   The federal legislation enacted in 1933 that provided emergency relief to homeowners through creation of the Home Owners' Loan Corporation to refinance or purchase existing home mortgages. The Act also authorized the creation of federally chartered and supervised savings associations.

homestead association   The name used by some state-chartered savings institutions in the state of Louisiana.

household   The persons residing in a discrete housing unit with access to either the outside or a public area; called a family when members are related by blood or law.

Housing and Urban Development Act   The federal legislation enacted in 1968 that gave federal associations the authority to invest in mobile home and home equipment loans. The law also expanded the authority of federal associations to issue a wide variety of savings plans, notes, bonds and debentures.

HUD   *See* Department of Housing and Urban Development.

I

implied warranty   An unwritten assurance that a product is fit for consumption. Under the 1976 amendments to the Uniform Commercial Code, the lender assumes the role of the seller in being responsible for the implied warranty. *See also* holder-in-due-course rule.

improved real estate   The real estate on which there is a structure (or structures) to be used for home or business purposes or both.

improvement lien   *See* special assessment.

income approach to value   The process of estimating the market value of a property by comparing the net rental income the property would produce over its remaining effective life with the yields on other kinds of investments with comparable risks.

income property loan   *See* commercial mortgage loan.

income statement   The financial statement that contains a summary of a business' financial operations for a particular period. It shows the net profit or loss for a period by stating the company's revenues and expenses.

independent audit   An examination of financial statements conducted by an "independent" CPA according to generally accepted auditing standards (GAAS) for the purpose of expressing an opinion on their fair presentation in accordance with generally accepted accounting principles (GAAP).

index   A numerical figure used in economics that describes relative changes in some quantity; e.g., the consumer price index. Adjustable mortgage loan interest rates often vary from period to period based on the movement of a specified index.

index of leading economic indicators   A composite of 12 economic measurements compiled by the Commerce Department to aid in predicting likely changes in the economy as a whole.

indirect loan   A loan originated by a dealer, retailer or seller of goods and services to finance the purchase of those goods and services and transferred to a third party. The loan is an indirect loan between the party to whom it is transferred and the borrower.

indirect origination   The purchase of a ready-made loan from a source other than a regular lender (such as a subdivision contractor or a mobile home or home improvement dealer), usually as part of an ongoing business relationship between the financial institution and the seller. *See also* loan origination.

individual account 1. A type of account ownership in which the account is owned and controlled by one individual. 2. A term used to describe account ownership by a natural person or persons as distinguished from ownership by a corporation or other legal entity.

Individual Retirement Account (IRA) A tax-deferred, trusteed deposit account into which certain eligible individuals contribute funds for retirement up to annual contribution limits. Approved vehicles for IRAs include deposit accounts and certificates at financial institutions, insurance annuities, mutual fund offerings and certain self-managed securities accounts at stock brokerage firms.

inflation An economic condition in which the purchasing power of the dollar decreases; a rise in the general level of prices. *See also* deflation.

inheritance tax waiver A release, signed by the appropriate state taxing official, relinquishing any claim of the state to the assets of an estate, or a portion thereof, under consideration.

insolvent 1. A state or condition of being unable to pay debts when they are due. 2. The condition wherein an entity's liabilities exceed its assets.

installment credit plan A repayment plan in which payments are scheduled at regular intervals; e.g., monthly, quarterly or semiannually, and must be continued until the full amount of the loan is satisfied. It allows consumers to obtain or enjoy the benefits of goods and services while paying for them in small amounts over a specified period of time.

installment debt *See* installment credit plan.

insufficient funds A term used to indicate that the drawer's deposit balance is less than the amount of a check presented for payment. Also known as not sufficient funds, abbreviated NSF.

insurance The indemnification against loss from a specific hazard or peril.

insurance fund The funds reserved in the Federal Deposit Insurance Corporation's (FDIC's) two subfunds, the Bank Insurance Fund (BIF) and Savings Association Fund (SAIF), to offset any claims made by depositors of defaulted member institutions.

insured institution An institution whose deposit accounts are insured by the Federal Deposit Insurance Corporation or some other governmental account-insuring agency.

intangible asset An item, owned by a business entity, that has value but no physical characteristics; for example, patents, copyrights and goodwill. *See also* goodwill.

liquidity A measure of the ability of a business, individual or institution to convert assets to cash without significant loss at a particular point in time.

liquidity risk The threat of not being able to liquidate an investment conveniently and at a reasonable price.

living trust A trust that transfers control of funds or property from a grantor to a trustee who distributes the income according to the terms of the trust agreement; known as a living trust because it is operative during the lifetime of the grantor.

load fund A class of mutual fund in which a sales commission is charged when a purchaser buys shares. *See also* no load fund.

loan A sum of money advanced to individuals, businesses, government units or others, to be repaid with or without interest as set forth in the accompanying bond, note or other evidence of indebtedness.

loan application A written or oral request for an extension of credit, which is made in accordance with procedures established by a lender (creditor) for the type of credit requested. Also, the form on which pertinent data about the request are recorded.

loan application register A register that lists all loan applications taken by a lending institution. Under the Fair Lending Practices Regulations, as amended in 1980, regulated institutions must keep separate registers for mortgage loans, mobile home loans, home improvement loans and equipment loans. Information to be entered in the register includes property location and data, applicant information, loan terms and loan disposition.

loan closing The process that brings a loan into legal existence, including the signing of all loan documents, their delivery to the appropriate parties and the disbursing of at least some of the loan proceeds.

loan fee The initial service charge to the borrower for placing a loan on the records of an institution; also called a loan origination fee, premium or initial servicing fee.

loan information sheet A listing of loans being offered for sale in secondary market transactions, showing principal balance, term, loan-to-value ratio and other items.

loan origination The steps taken by a lending institution up to the time a loan is placed on its books, including solicitation of applications, application processing and loan closing. *See also* indirect origination.

loan origination fee A one-time charge based on the amount of a loan and paid at settlement. The fee is usually paid by buyers, but may be assumed by a seller.

loan participation agreement A contract, in secondary market transactions, under which the seller agrees to supply, and the buyer agrees to purchase, interests in blocks of loans at a future date; the agreement sets forth the conditions for individual transactions, and the rights and responsibilities of both parties. *See also* participation.

loan policy The written guidelines detailing the methods and procedures for accomplishing a financial institution's goals and objectives. It details the types of loans an institution makes, the employees who may take loan applications for the institution and the procedures for accepting and processing an application.

loan portfolio The total of all the loans that a financial institution, or other lender, holds at a given time.

loan proceeds The net amount of funds that a financial institution disburses at the direction of a borrower and that the borrower thereafter owes.

loan processing The steps taken by an institution from the time a loan application is received to the time it is approved, including taking an application, credit investigation, evaluation of the loan terms and other steps.

loan servicing The steps taken to maintain a loan, from the time it is made until the last payment is received and the loan instruments are canceled. Steps may include billing the borrower, collecting payments and escrowing real estate tax and fire and casualty insurance payments.

loan settlement statement A document, prepared for and presented to the borrower at a loan closing, showing all disbursements to be made from the loan proceeds.

loan terms The loan amount, interest rate and length of time granted for repayment of the loan.

loan-to-value ratio The ratio, usually expressed as a percentage, that the principal amount of a mortgage loan bears to the mortgaged property's appraised value, as "an 80% loan" or "a 95% loan limit."

loan underwriting The process of determining the risks inherent in a particular loan and establishing suitable terms and conditions for the loan.

loans in process General ledger account from which loan funds usually are disbursed.

loan underwriting standards A written summary of a financial institution's lending policies and procedures; it also may cover the types of loan programs that the institution offers. The underwriting standards must be made available to members of the public upon request. *See also* fair lending practices regulations.

loan workout   The plan of action initiated by the lender that involves taking steps with the borrower to resolve a problem loan.

local check   A check drawn on a bank located within the same Federal Reserve check-processing region as the depository institution where the check is presented. The check-processing region can usually be determined by the routing number printed on the check.

location information   The information defined by the Fair Debt Collection Practices Act to protect borrowers' financial privacy. The Act limits the amount of information that loan collectors can obtain from third parties when trying to find a borrower. For example, a collector cannot obtain the address of the borrower's place of residence or the borrower's place of employment from a third party.

lock box   A post office box to which customers mail payments to an institution. Payments are picked up for processing by either the institution itself or another institution that has contracted to provide these processing services.

long-term asset   An asset whose economic life is expected to exceed one business cycle, normally greater than one year.

long-term debt   A debt that is due after more than one year.

L

lump-sum distribution   The withdrawal of an individual's pension benefits or retirement savings in the form of a single payment or lump sum. All, or any part, of a lump-sum distribution can be used to establish a rollover IRA. *See also* allowable distributions.

M

magnetic ink character recognition (MICR) The electronic reading of machine-legible characters printed in magnetic ink, such as those appearing on checks.

manufactured home A dwelling that is wholly or partly built in a factory and then delivered whole, or in parts, to the site where it is assembled.

manufactured home loan A loan to an individual for the purchase of a manufactured home, secured by the lender's claim on the home. The most common type of manufactured home is the mobile home.

margin **1.** The difference between the interest rates charged on loans and the rate that the institution pays to raise lending funds. Also known as spread. **2.** The percentage of the purchase price of a security that must be put up in cash.

marketable securities Those securities that have available a ready, active market.

market data approach to value The method used in appraising to determine the market value of a property by comparing the property being appraised to similar properties recently sold. Comparisons are made regarding such qualities as the price paid, financing arrangements and physical attributes.

market research The process of planning, gathering, analyzing and interpreting the facts about a market; about the product or service being marketed; and about the past, present and potential customers for that product or service.

market segments Consumer groups identified by their demographic or psychographic profiles, their wants or needs, or their response to advertising and promotional activities.

market value The highest monetary price a property can be expected to bring if the following conditions are present: (1) buyer and seller are normally motivated and free of undue pressure; (2) both are well-informed or well-advised and act prudently in their best interests; (3) reasonable time is allowed to test the property on the open market; (4) payment is made in cash or financed at terms usual for both the location and type of property. Market value also contemplates the sale's consummation and passing of full title from seller to buyer.

market-value accounting A system of accounting in which assets and liabilities are accounted for with a dollar value at their current, or relatively current, price in the marketplace. Market value ignores historical costs and will fluctuate according to economic conditions.

master plan insurance   A form of coverage that insures a financial institution against loss resulting from certain types of damage to a security property, whether or not the borrower maintains any coverage.

maturity   1. The period of time for which credit, an insurance contract, or a mortgage loan is written. 2. The dates on which certain types of investments may be redeemed at face value. 3. The amount of time one must wait before realizing the rate of return expected when the investment was made.

maturity amount   The value of an investment at the end of its economic life.

mechanic's lien   A lien, created by statute in most states, in favor of persons who have performed work or furnished material used in the construction of a building or other improvement; also called a materialmen's lien.

members   The group of savers and borrowers in a mutual savings association who elect directors, amend the bylaws, approve any basic corporate change of policy or organization and, in general, possess most of the rights of ownership that stockholders have in a stock corporation.

merger   A business consolidation in which two or more corporations create a new corporation by unifying their capital, liabilities and assets.

metropolitan statistical area (MSA)   A geographic unit composed of one or more counties around a central city, or urbanized area, with 50,000 or more inhabitants. Contiguous counties are included if they have close social and economic links with the area's population nucleus. Formerly known as standard metropolitan statistical areas (SMSAs).

M

MICR   *See* magnetic ink character recognition.

mobile home   *See* manufactured home.

modification agreement   An agreement between a lender and borrower that alters permanently one or more of the terms—interest rate, number of years allowed for repayment, monthly payment amount and the like—of an existing mortgage loan.

monetary policy   The government regulation of the supply of money and credit; usually assigned to the Federal Reserve Board. *See also* fiscal policy.

money   A generally accepted medium of exchange, measure of value or means of payment.

money laundering   The transfer of illegally obtained funds between accounts in different financial institutions to obscure the origin of the funds. Penalties to financial institutions engaged in these activities are outlined in the Bank Secrecy Act.

money market   The common term for the mechanism whereby loanable funds are traded in the form of short-term debt securities.

money market deposit account (MMDA) A federally insured savings deposit account offered by financial institutions and designed to be competitive with money market mutual funds. It has no legal minimum balance or interest rate restrictions; however, financial institutions typically set their own. The MMDA has limitations on the number of certain transactions allowed per month. Because of these limitations, MMDAs are not normally considered transaction accounts and are not subject to federal reserve requirements. *See also* demand deposit; money market mutual fund; Regulation D; savings deposit; transaction account.

money market mutual fund (MMMF) A mutual fund that invests in short-term obligations only, such as commercial paper or Treasury bills. The yields on these investments fluctuate due to varying interest rates and the continuously changing investment portfolios. Money market mutual funds are not federally insured.

money order An order purchased from a financial institution, the U.S. Postal Service or a commercial company to pay a sum of money specified by the purchaser to a party named by the purchaser. Because the funds being transferred in this way have already been paid to the firm or government body issuing the order, anyone who cashes the order after properly identifying the payee is sure of reimbursement; thus, a money order is easily converted to cash anywhere in the nation.

mortgage A legal document by which real property is pledged as security for the repayment of a loan. The pledge ends when the debt is discharged.

mortgage-backed security A bond-type investment security representing an undivided interest in a pool of mortgages.

mortgage banker An individual or corporation that deals in mortgage loans by originating the loans and then selling them to investors, with servicing retained by the seller-banker for the life of a loan in exchange for a fee.

mortgage bond A bond that is secured by real property.

mortgage-equity analysis A method of estimating value by dividing the investment in a property into its mortgage and equity components and capitalizing.

mortgage life insurance An insurance policy on the life of a borrower that repays an outstanding mortgage debt upon death of the insured.

mortgage pool A number of mortgages combined and issued as a single security by financial institutions. Repayments from the pool are used to pay off the security.

mortgagee The institution, group or individual that lends money on the security of pledged real estate; commonly called the lender.

mortgagor   The owner of real estate who pledges property as security for the repayment of a debt; commonly called the borrower.

MSA   *See* metropolitan statistical area.

multifamily   A structure defined in government statistics as containing more than four dwelling units; or, sometimes, used to describe a unit itself.

municipal bond   The obligation of a state or local government agency to repay with interest a sum of money borrowed for municipal purposes, such as the building of low-income housing, improving streets or building bridges. Commonly called municipals.

mutual fund   A financial corporation that invests funds obtained from the sale of shares of its own stock in the securities of other corporations. Dividends paid to shareholders are based on the earnings of the securities, minus expenses. Also called an open-end investment company.

mutual institution   A savings institution that issues no capital stock, but is owned and controlled solely by its savers and borrowers, who are called members. Members do not share in profits, because a mutual institution operates in such a way that it makes no "profit," but members exercise other ownership rights.

mutual savings bank   A financial institution incorporated for the purposes of: (1) providing a safe place for individuals to save and (2) investing those savings in mortgage loans, stocks, bonds and other securities.

N

National Credit Union Share Insurance Fund (NCUSIF) A fund that insures deposits in federally chartered credit unions. The National Credit Union Administration (NCUA), a federal agency, administers the NCUSIF, which provides share account coverage similar to that provided by the Federal Deposit Insurance Corporation (FDIC) for deposits.

National Flood Insurance Program A program that provides flood insurance at affordable rates through a federal subsidy. In return for this subsidy, communities in designated flood hazard areas must administer local measures that aid in flood prevention.

negative amortization A mortgage repayment plan in which the borrower makes less-than-interest-only payments on the amount of money borrowed during part of the payment term. Unpaid interest is accrued on the outstanding loan balance, causing the loan balance to increase instead of decrease.

negotiable A term meaning assignable or transferable, in lieu of money, in the ordinary course of business.

negotiable instrument A written order or promise to transfer money from one party to another by delivery or by endorsement and delivery, and without formal assignment; when the transfer has been made, the receiving party has full legal title. A negotiable instrument ordinarily is in the form of a check, draft or bill of exchange, promissory note or acceptance.

net income The difference between the revenues earned and the expenses incurred by a corporation in a given period.

net savings inflow The change in an institution's savings account balances over a given period, determined by subtracting withdrawals during the period; also called net savings gain or net savings receipts. When interest credited to accounts during the period is excluded, the resulting figure customarily is referred to as net new savings.

net worth The sum of all reserve accounts (except specific or valuation reserves), retained earnings, permanent stock, mutual capital certificates, securities that constitute permanent equity capital in accordance with generally accepted accounting principles, and any other nonwithdrawable accounts of an insured institution. Generally, the net worth of an individual or business is the difference between total assets and total liabilities. *See also* asset and liability mix.

no load fund A class of mutual fund in which no load fee (sales commission) is charged when a purchaser buys shares. *See also* load fund.

nonamortized loan A loan in which the periodic payments are sufficient to cover only the interest due; the principal is not reduced.

nonbank bank A financial service institution that either accepts demand deposits or makes commercial loans, but does not do both. Also known as a consumer bank.

nonfiling insurance A type of insurance that insures the institution against a loss that results from unintentional errors or omissions in the filing or recording of a security interest.

nonlocal check A check drawn on a bank located outside the Federal Reserve check-processing region of the depository institution where the check is presented. The check-processing region can usually be determined by the routing number printed on the check.

nonoperating expense The expenses resulting from nonrecurring financial transactions that do not result from the regular and ordinary operations of a firm (e.g., expense of maintaining real estate owned or a loss from the sale of real estate owned).

nonoperating revenue The revenue derived from nonrecurring financial transactions that do not result from the regular or ordinary operations of a firm (e.g., profit on the sale of real estate owned).

no-par stock A stock issued with no face value.

notary public A public officer authorized to attest to the signing of documents (such as deeds or mortgages) requiring certification. The person signs and affixes a seal to the document.

N

note *See* promissory note.

notice account A savings or time deposit account on which the customer agrees to give the institution a specified notice before making a withdrawal. As long as the customer gives the agreed notice, the funds earn a higher interest rate than that paid on other regular accounts; insufficient notice for a withdrawal may incur a penalty. *See also* penalty clause.

novation The substitution of a new obligation for an old one between the same or different parties.

NOW account A savings account from which the account holder can withdraw funds by writing a negotiable order of withdrawal (NOW) payable to a third party. Interest may be paid on the NOW accounts. *See also* NOW account drafts; transaction accounts.

NOW account drafts The negotiable instruments written on a NOW account to make third-party payments. May also be referred to as a check. *See also* NOW account.

NSF *See* insufficient funds.

O

OCC *See* Office of the Comptroller of the Currency.

odd lot A block of shares smaller than a round lot (a multiple of 100) and usually traded at one time.

Office of the Comptroller of the Currency (OCC) The part of the national banking system that supervises the operations of national banks, including trust activities and overseas operations. The Comptroller, as administrator of national banks, is responsible for executing laws relating to national banks and can officially issue rules and regulations governing their organization and operations. The Comptroller also serves as one of five members of the FDIC board. *See also* FDIC; BIF; SAIF.

Office of Thrift Supervision (OTS) An office in the Department of the Treasury created by Title III of FIRREA to charter, regulate, supervise, and examine federally chartered and state-chartered savings associations and savings and loan holding companies. All OTS regulations and policies are to be no less stringent than those established by the OCC for national banks. *See also* DOTS; OCC; FIRREA.

offsite improvements The improvements, in land development, that are off the development site, such as roads and utility services to the site, and that enhance the value of the development.

onsite improvements The improvements within the boundaries of a land development, such as streets, sidewalks and utility services, that increase the value of the development.

on-us checks The term used by a financial institution to refer to checks drawn on itself. A check is considered an on-us check when it is cashed over the counter by the payer bank.

on-us transaction A transaction in which an institution's customer presents a check that is drawn on that institution, or transacts business through an automated teller machine owned by that institution.

open-end credit An available (open) line of credit up to a predetermined amount (dollar credit limit). Consumers can draw against their line of credit without making specific arrangements for each purchase. Consumers also can make payments that most closely reflect their financial capabilities at a particular time. As the loan balance is reduced, the available credit increases to the predetermined limit. The line of credit remains available until either the borrower or lender cancels it.

open-end investment company *See* mutual fund.

operating expense   A charge incurred as a result of the customary savings and lending business of an institution, excluding interest on borrowed money, interest paid to savers and taxes. Major operating expense items are compensation and related costs, office occupancy, fixtures and equipment, advertising, federal insurance premiums, and professional and supervisory fees.

operating income   The receipts arising from the customary savings and lending business of an institution; sometimes called gross operating income. Major operating income items are interest on loans and other investments, and loan fees and charges.

operating leverage   The degree to which fixed costs comprise a firm's total costs. *See also* financial leverage.

operations analysis   A system of analyzing a business's operations in order to establish norms, appraise efficiency, improve operations and reduce costs.

origination fee   A consideration (fee), other than the average interest provided by the loan contract, received by an institution for or in connection with the acquisition, making, refinancing or modification of a loan, plus any consideration received for making a loan commitment, whether or not an actual loan follows such commitment.

OTC   *See* over-the-counter.

OTS   *See* Office of Thrift Supervision.

outstanding check   A check that has not yet been presented for payment to the financial institution on which it was drawn.

overdraft   A draft or check written for an amount that exceeds the balance in a customer's account.

overdraft protection   A line of credit on which customers can write checks for an amount over and above the balance in their checking accounts. *See also* check credit.

overimprovement   The condition of a property, in appraising, wherein the value of the site plus the cost of the building's improvements have considerably more value than most of the nearby sites.

over-the-counter (OTC)   A means of trading shares of a company not listed on an organized stock exchange.

ownership   The state of holding a lawful claim or title to property.

P

par value 1. A value that has been assigned to a share of stock by the corporate charter. This value has nothing to do with the market value of the share. 2. The value of a bond at maturity. *See also* face value.

partial release An institution's relinquishment of its claim to some part of the real property that secures a mortgage loan.

partially amortizing loan A loan in which the periodic payments cover all of the interest due, but only part of the principal; a sizable balance remains when the loan matures.

participation 1. The partial ownership interest in a mortgage or package of mortgages. 2. The origination, by two or more lenders, of a single (often large) mortgage loan. *See also* loan participation agreement.

participation loan A loan made or owned by more than one lender; the joint investors share profits and losses in proportion to their ownership shares.

partnership A form of business organization in which two or more persons join in a commercial or business enterprise, sharing profits and risks as they have contractually agreed. No stock is issued, and the partnership exists only as long as all partners stay in the business; a change of partner necessitates the formation of a new partnership.

passbook The evidence of ownership of a savings account; the customer's record of transactions on the account, such as deposits, withdrawals and earnings received.

passbook account *See* regular savings account.

passbook loan *See* savings account loan.

pass-through security A security representing an interest in a pool of mortgages in which mortgage repayments are passed through to the security-holder.

payee The party to whom a check is payable.

payer The person who pays, or is to make payment of, a check.

payment cap A restriction placed upon the extent to which the monthly payment can change during the term of an adjustable rate mortgage loan or from one adjustment period to another.

payoff The complete repayment of loan principal, interest and any other sums due; payoff occurs either over the full term of the loan or through prepayments.

payoff statement A formal statement prepared when a loan payoff is contemplated, showing the current status of the loan account, all sums due and the daily rate of interest. Also called a letter of demand.

payout The disbursement of loan funds to a borrower. In construction lending, the incremental disbursement of loan funds contingent upon the completion of a specified portion of a structure, such as a foundation, roof, etc.

payroll savings plan An arrangement whereby an employee authorizes his or her employer to deduct specified wages or salary each pay period and to forward that amount to a financial institution for deposit in the employee's savings account.

p/e ratio *See* price-earnings ratio.

penalty clause **1.** A clause in a promissory note specifying a penalty for late payments. **2.** A clause in a savings certificate specifying a penalty for premature withdrawal from such an account.

pension fund A fund set up to collect regular premiums from individuals and their employers, invest those funds safely and profitably, and pay out a monthly income when an individual reaches retirement age.

period certain A predetermined amount of time during which a participant receives allowable distributions from an IRA. A period certain may be any length of time so long as the period is less than the participant's life expectancy. *See also* allowable distributions.

period of redemption The length of time during which a defaulted mortgagor may reclaim the title and possession of his or her property by paying the debt secured by the property.

permanent insurance A form of life insurance incorporating a savings or investment feature. The full death benefit will continue to remain in force when the policy matures, without the necessity for any further premium payment, as compared with term insurance, which lapses upon nonpayment of the premium.

permanent lender A lender that provides long-term financing for projects after construction has been completed.

permanent loan A long-term loan or mortgage that is fully amortized and extended for a period of not less than 10 years.

personal check A check drawn on a depository institution by an individual against that individual's own funds.

P

personal identification number (PIN)   A secret number or code used by an account holder to authorize a transaction or obtain information regarding that person's account. The PIN may be used in conjunction with a plastic card to insure that the person activating an automatic device with a plastic card is the individual to whom the card was issued.

personal loan   An unsecured loan usually made for the purpose of debt consolidation, vacation or the purchase of durable goods.

personal property   The movable items that a person owns, either tangible, such as furniture and other merchandise, or intangible, such as stocks and bonds.

personal savings   The balance remaining after deducting expenditures for goods and services from the after-tax income of individuals and families.

physical deterioration   The loss of property value due to the actual decay of the physical components of real estate.

PIN   *See* personal identification number.

planned unit development (PUD)   A land development project planned as an entity; building units are generally grouped into clusters, allowing an appreciable amount of land for open space. Generally more than one housing type or land use is included, and the project is generally subjected to various types of review and approval by the controlling governmental unit.

point   An amount equal to 1% of the principal amount of an investment or note. Points are a one-time charge assessed by the lender to increase the yield on the mortgage loan to a competitive position with other types of investments.

point-of-sale, place-of-business (POS or POB)   The retail firm where an electronic funds transfer system (EFTS) computer terminal is located.

pooling of interest method   A method of accounting used when combining two or more institutions in which assets, liabilities and net worth of the combined institutions are recorded at their book value. Adjustments are made when institutions use different accounting methods for recording assets and liabilities.

portfolio   A list, or grouping, of the income-earnings assets of an individual or a financial institution.

portfolio yield   The return on a collection of investments assembled to meet one or more investment goals. Examples include mortgage and consumer loan portfolios that an institution may own. An institution subtracts its cost of funds from its portfolio yield to determine its spread. *See also* cost of funds; yield; rate of return.

postal money order   An instrument, like a check, sold by United States post offices for payment of a specified sum of money to the individual or firm designated by the purchaser.

posting   The process of transferring journal entries to the general ledger.

power of attorney   A document that authorizes one person to legally act in place of another person under specified conditions for specific purposes.

power of sale clause   A clause in a mortgage document that gives the institution the right to sell the property at a public auction without a prior court judgment.

preauthorized payment   A system established by written agreement whereby a financial institution is authorized by the customer to debit his or her checking account for a monthly loan payment. The institution is instructed to honor such debits, whether paper check, magnetic tape or punch card.

preferred stock   A stock yielding a fixed-dollar income. The stockholder has a claim to earnings and assets before the holder of common stock, but after the claim of bonds. *See also* stock.

premium   **1.** A product given free or sold at a fraction of its real price; offered as an inducement to the public to open or add to a deposit account. **2.** The price paid for a contract of insurance. **3.** A fee charged for the granting of a loan. **4.** The amount above the face value of an investment.

prepayment clause   A clause in a promissory note stipulating the amount a borrower may pay ahead of schedule without penalty, as well as the penalty for larger prepayments.

present value   A representation of the current value of a sum that is to be received at some time in the future.

P

price-earnings (p/e) ratio   A ratio often used by investors to determine the value of a stock. The ratio is the market value of a share divided by its earnings for the previous year.

prime rate   The interest rate charged by leading banks for loans to their most secure customers.

principal   The amount of money borrowed, as distinguished from interest or charges.

principal balance   The portion of the loan amount not repaid, exclusive of interest and any other charges.

private mortgage insurance An insurance policy, offered by a private company, that protects a lender against loss up to policy limits (customarily 20% to 25% of the loan amount) on a defaulted mortgage loan. Its use usually is limited to loans with a high loan-to-value ratio; the borrower pays the premiums.

probate The process of admitting a will to record, resolving questions that arise in estate administration and approving the accounts of an executor or of an administrator. Also, an order of court judging a will to be valid and ordering it to be recorded.

pro forma statements The projected income statement and balance sheet for some specified future period.

pro rata A Latin term meaning in proportion to; e.g., the amount charged to each homeowner to cover the cost of a special assessment.

profit and loss statement *See* statement of operations; income statement.

profit center accounting A method that identifies for each operating function its contribution to the profit of the institution as a whole.

promissory note A written promise to pay a stipulated sum of money to a specified party under conditions mutually agreed upon. Also called a note, installment note, promise or bond.

property A piece of real estate; or, generally, something owned or possessed.

property and casualty insurance A type of insurance that provides for the replacement of or compensation for lost, stolen, damaged or destroyed property.

property assessment The valuation of real property for tax purposes.

prospectus A document detailing investment objectives and other important characteristics of a security, and the key characteristics of the issuer, including its management and financial position. Under SEC regulations, the prospectus (1) must contain the no-approval clause, stating that the SEC has not approved or disapproved of the issue; and (2) must be provided to all prospective investors.

proxy 1. The authority or power to act for another. 2. A document giving such authority. 3. The person authorized to act for another.

public unit account A deposit account that contains the funds of a state, county, municipality or other government unit.

PUD *See* planned unit development.

purchase method of accounting   A method of accounting used in institution mergers whereby the assets and liabilities of the acquired institution are recorded at their fair value. The direct acquisition costs are included in the cost of the acquired institution. Goodwill is recorded for the excess of cost over identifiable assets minus liabilities. As of the acquisition date, the acquired institution's net worth is eliminated.

put option   The option to sell a given amount of a commodity at a specified price during a specified period of time. *See also* call option.

P

Q

qualified opinion The second paragraph in an independent auditor's report, which states that the financial statements present fairly the financial position of a firm according to generally accepted accounting principles applied on a basis consistent with that of the previous year *except* for a particular matter.

qualified pension plan A classification given by the Internal Revenue Service to a retirement or profit-sharing plan that meets certain requirements; also known as Section 401(a) plan. This classification means only that the plan qualifies for favorable tax treatment.

qualified retirement plan A private retirement plan that meets Internal Revenue Service guidelines and regulations and offers tax advantages to businesses and individuals.

Qualified Thrift Lender (QTL) Test The test for asset standards, mandated by FIRREA, that all savings associations are required to maintain. As of July 1, 1991, the asset standards required by the test are as follows: Seventy percent of portfolio assets shall be qualified housing-related investments, with at least 55 percent for residential finance, and up to 15 percent for residential finance-related investments, of which up to 5 percent may consist of consumer loans. Failure to pass the Qualified Thrift Lender Test will subject the association to significant business restrictions. *See also* FIRREA; DOTS.

quit claim deed A deed by which the owner of real estate conveys to another whatever title or interest he or she has to a property, but which makes no representation that the property is free from encumbrances except those created by the owner. *See also* deed.

R

rate of return The measure of profitability of an investment expressed as a percentage rate of gain or loss per year on the amount invested. Also known as return on investment. *See also* yield.

rating A formal opinion in securities trading given by an outside professional service on the credit reputation of a bond issuer and the investment quality of its securities. This opinion is expressed in letter values (AAA, Baa-1, etc.).

real accounts The accounts—asset, liability, reserve and capital—whose balances are not canceled out at the end of an accounting period but are carried over to the next period. These accounts appear on the post-closing trial balance and the statement of condition (balance sheet). Sometimes called permanent accounts.

real assets The tangible assets, in contrast to financial assets or securities. Included are real estate, land, gold, coins, stamps, art and antiques.

real estate A parcel of land and any buildings or other objects permanently affixed to it. The term "real estate" refers to the interests, benefits and rights inherent in the ownership of real property. For all practical purposes, the same as real property. *See also* personal property; real property.

real estate mortgage investment conduit (REMIC) A residential and commercial security vehicle, made possible by the Tax Reform Act of 1986, that allows issuers to sell mortgages outright while offering investors multiple classes of securities from which to choose. The vehicle offers issuers both balance sheet and tax advantages. *See also* collateralized mortgage obligation.

real estate investment trust (REIT) An unincorporated trust or association, managed by one or more trustees for the benefit of a number of beneficiaries, that invests in real estate such as office buildings, apartment houses and shopping centers.

real estate owned (REO) The real estate owned by a lending institution as the result of default on the part of a borrower.

Real Estate Settlement Procedures Act (RESPA) A federal law, enacted in 1974 and subsequently amended, that requires lenders to provide home mortgage borrowers with information of known or estimated settlement costs. *See also* good faith estimate; Uniform Settlement Statement; Regulation Z.

Q
R

real property   An area of land and any buildings or other objects that are permanently affixed to it. The term "real property" refers to the interests, benefits and rights inherent in the ownership of real estate. That which is not real property is personal property. *See also* personal property; real estate.

real time   A term that pertains to the processing of information or transactions as they actually occur.

recession   A period of reduced economic activity during which the level of unemployment rises, the means of production becomes increasingly idle and general prosperity lags.

reconciliation   The process of analyzing the cause of differences between two related records. The most frequent use in accounting is bank statement reconciliation during which statements from depository banks are analyzed and compared with the institution's cash account.

records of original entry   The general journal and special journals (e.g., cash receipts and disbursements journals) that list and serve as written records of the firm's transactions in chronological order. All transactions are analyzed and recorded in one of these journals before being posted in the general ledger account. *See also* cash journals.

recourse   The right to demand payment from the maker or endorser of a negotiable instrument.

redemption of accounts   The power of a mutual savings institution to buy back the savings accounts of its members by paying their full withdrawal value.

redemption period   *See* period of redemption.

redemption right   A defaulted mortgagor's right to redeem his or her property after default and court judgment, both before and after sale of the property. *See also* equitable right of redemption; statutory right of redemption.

red herring   A preliminary prospectus used by companies during the term between the Securities Exchange Commission authorization of a security and the date on which the issuer is authorized to sell.

redlining   The refusal of a business to extend credit to, lend to, insure, or otherwise assume some financial risk involving a piece of real property or place of business located in a high-risk geographical area, most often a declining inner-city neighborhood; alternatively, fees for financial services in a redlined area may be set prohibitively high.

REFCORP   *See* Resolution Funding Corporation.

refinancing   The repayment of a debt from the proceeds of a new loan using the same property as security.

registered bond   A bond on which the company automatically mails interest payments to the bond's owner. The bond also is registered in the name of the owner by the issuing company. *See also* coupon bond.

registered investment advisor   A person who is registered with the Securities and Exchange Commission and who provides advice on a fee basis regarding the purchase or sale of securities.

registered representative   An individual who handles the buying and selling of securities for customers and who is licensed through the National Association of Securities Dealers and sponsored by a broker-dealer.

regular mortgage   The legal document used in most states to pledge real estate as security for the repayment of a debt. Also known in some states as a deed of trust.

regular savings account   A savings account that typically requires a low minimum balance, no minimum term, no specified minimum deposit, and no notice or penalty for withdrawals. Also called passbook account.

Regulation B   The Federal Reserve regulation that specifies nondiscrimination requirements lenders must follow when granting credit. Also known as the Equal Credit Opportunity Act of 1974.

Regulation CC   The Federal Reserve regulation that establishes time schedules for maximum check holds and provides safeguards to minimize risk of loss to institutions in situations involving new and existing accounts. Also known as the Expedited Funds Availability Act of 1987.

Regulation D   The Federal Reserve regulation requiring depository institutions to maintain reserves to facilitate implementation of the Federal Reserve System's monetary policy. Institutions must maintain reserves for deposits in demand deposit and transaction accounts, including noninterest bearing checking accounts and other checks (such as certified, cashiers and traveler's checks and money orders) that are primary obligations of the issuing institution. *See also* demand deposit; Federal funds interest rate; transaction account.

Regulation E   The Federal Reserve regulation that establishes the basic rights, liabilities, and responsibilities of consumers who use electronic money transfer services and of financial institutions that offer these services. Also known as the Electronic Fund Transfer Act of the Consumer Credit Protection Act.

Regulation J   The Federal Reserve regulation that specifies the rules under which the Fed will accept, clear and settle for items collected through the Federal Reserve System.

Regulation Q   A 1933 Federal Reserve Board ruling that made commercial banks subject to rate controls for interest on savings accounts.

R

Regulation Z   The title of the Federal Reserve Board's regulations implementing the Consumer Credit Protection Act for all lenders. *See also* Truth-in-Lending Act; Real Estate Settlement Procedures Act.

rehabilitation loan   A loan to finance substantial alteration, repair or improvement of primary residential property.

reinstatement   A complete resolution of a mortgage delinquency by the borrower, thus restoring the loan to current status.

REIT   *See* real estate investment trust.

release   The discharge of property from a mortgage lien; a written statement that an obligation has been satisfied.

release deed   *See* satisfaction of mortgage.

REMIC   *See* real estate mortgage investment conduit.

REO   *See* real estate owned.

reorganization   The distribution of borrowers' assets to creditors, according to a plan constructed by the borrowers or creditors, in which creditors classify their claims in a way most beneficial to them. Also called Chapter 11 bankruptcy.

replacement cost   The current cost of producing, on a site, similar (but not identical) improvements possessing equal utility with the original improvements. *See also* reproduction cost.

repossession   A remedy available to lenders whereby personal property used as security for a delinquent debt is acquired and disposed of for the purpose of repaying the loan in whole or in part.

reproduction cost   The current cost of duplicating the improvements on a site with identical (or effectively identical) materials. *See also* replacement cost.

repurchase agreement   **1.** An agreement between a financial institution and a customer where the institution sells a portion of a government security it owns, agrees to pay a specified interest rate and to repurchase that security, plus accrued interest, at a specified time. (Such investments are not federally insured.) Commonly called a repo. **2.** An agreement used in consumer lending to establish the indirect lender's right to seek loan repayment from the dealer if conditions set forth in the retail installment contract are not met. The dealer refers to merchants who originate the retail installment contract with the buyer of the merchandise.

required reserves   A specified amount of cash on deposit and immediately available from reserve accounts at Federal Reserve banks, the minimum amount of which is prescribed by the Federal Reserve's Regulation D. Institutions must maintain reserves for deposits in demand deposit and transaction accounts. The Federal Reserve requires depository institutions to maintain reserves to facilitate implementation of the Federal Reserve System's monetary policy and to enable institutions to maintain their ability to pay liabilities in cash. *See also* demand deposit; Federal funds interest rate; Regulation D; transaction account.

reserve for bad debts   A reserve account to which bad debt losses are charged. Under federal tax laws, savings institutions are allowed to build up such reserves by making tax-deductible allocations of earnings according to a specified formula.

reserves   The portion of earnings set aside to take care of any possible losses in the conduct of business; especially funds set aside to cover potential losses on loans or other investments.

residence   *See* domicile.

residential mortgage loan   A loan secured by real estate of one- to four-family dwellings.

Resolution Funding Corporation (REFCORP)   An instrumentality of the federal government created by Title V of FIRREA to provide funds to the Resolution Trust Corporation (RTC) for resolving failed savings associations. *See also* RTC; FIRREA.

Resolution Trust Corporation (RTC)   An instrumentality of the federal government created by Title V of FIRREA to manage and sell assets of insolvent savings institutions whose accounts were previously insured by the Federal Savings and Loan Insurance Corporation (FSLIC). The RTC's duties include acting as a conservator or receiver of an insured institution. The RTC Oversight Board and the Federal Deposit Insurance Corporation (FDIC) establish general policies and manage the RTC's duties. *See also* RTC Oversight Board; FDIC; FIRREA.

RESPA   *See* Real Estate Settlement Procedures Act.

R

restrictive endorsement   An endorsement that limits the negotiability of an instrument or contains a definite condition as to payment. It purports to preclude the endorsee from making any further transfer of the instrument. *See also* blank endorsement; endorsement.

retail banking   The banking services offered to the general public, including consumers and small businesses.

retail open charge credit   The credit extended to borrowers to acquire goods with the promise to pay the retailer in full usually within a 30-day period. The consumer usually pays no additional fees for the privilege of the delayed payment.

retail revolving credit   A credit purchase in which a customer is permitted to purchase goods or services by agreeing to make full payment for them within 25 to 30 days, or a monthly payment in which an interest charge for the privilege of using this type of credit is added.

retained earnings   The corporate profits that are neither paid out in cash dividends nor used to increase capital stock but are reinvested in the company.

retirement bond   A bond issued prior to May of 1982 by the United States government as part of an individual retirement savings program, also known as a Qualified Retirement Bond. *See also* retirement savings programs.

retirement savings programs   A general term relating to the three programs created by the Employee Retirement Income Security Act of 1974 (ERISA): IRAs, retirement annuities and retirement bonds.

return on average assets   A ratio used to measure the efficiency with which a business entity uses its assets. Return on average assets is expressed as a ratio:

$$\frac{\text{net income}}{\text{average total assets}}$$

(net of loans in process if a lending institution)

The higher the ratio (greater the return), the greater the efficiency.

return on average equity   A ratio used to measure a business entity's effectiveness in investing its net worth. Return on average equity is expressed as a ratio:

$$\frac{\text{net income}}{\text{average equity}}$$

The higher the ratio (greater the return), the more effective the investment.

return on investment   *See* rate of return.

revenue bond   A bond backed only by the revenue of the facility constructed with the funds it raised, such as an airport or turnpike. *See also* general obligation bond.

revenues   The earnings of a firm; the dollar amount received for goods sold or services rendered during a given time period.

reverse annuity mortgage A form of mortgage that enables homeowners to borrow, in monthly installments, against the equity in their homes. The payments to the homeowner are made by the lender or through the purchase of an annuity from an insurance company. Reverse annuity mortgages are especially beneficial for retired homeowners, who can use the monthly payments to help meet living expenses. *See also* annuity; mortgage.

revocable trust A trust in which the grantor reserves the right to annul the trust; if this is done, the trust property reverts back to the grantor. *See also* trust account.

right of foreclosure The right of the lending institution to take over property and close out the mortgagor's interest in it if the mortgagor violates the provisions of the mortgage or note.

right of rescission The right of consumers to cancel any credit transaction in which the collateral used to secure the transaction is their principal place of residence. The cancellation must occur within three business days from whichever of the following events occurs last: (1) the date of the transaction; or (2) the date on which the truth-in-lending disclosures are received; or (3) the date on which the notice of the right to cancel is received.

right of setoff The right of the creditor to commence judicial proceedings against a borrower, sell repossessed collateral or use other assets of the borrower to satisfy payment of the debt.

risk The probability of loss, or the degree of uncertainty, associated with the return on an investment.

robbery The taking by force, or the attempt to take by force, property, money or other things of value belonging to, or in the possession of, a person or a business.

rollover A distribution of the funds from a qualified retirement plan to a participant for the establishment of another qualified retirement savings plan.

round lot A block of shares, usually in multiples of 100, for trading on the exchanges.

routing and transit numbers The identification numbers that appear on each check or draft designating the institution and its location for purposes of facilitating the check-collection process.

RTC *See* Resolution Trust Corporation.

R

RTC Oversight Board   An instrumentality of the federal government created by Title V of FIRREA to establish general policies for the Resolution Trust Corporation (RTC), including procedures for case resolutions and for managing and selling assets of failed savings associations, and to oversee the RTC's activities. The Oversight Board consists of the following five members: the Secretary of the Treasury as chairperson; the Chairman of the Board of Governors of the Federal Reserve System; the Secretary of Housing and Urban Development; and two independent members appointed by the president, with Senate approval. *See also* RTC; FDIC.

Rule of 72   A method used to estimate the number of years required for compounding to double the original investment. Calculated by dividing 72 by the interest rate earned on an investment.

Rule of 78s   A method of recognizing add-on interest by using predetermined factors to calculate the portion of total interest earned for the period. A declining ratio is applied to a fixed-loan amount to determine interest earned for the period. Also known as sum-of-the-digits method.

rules of the class   The terms and conditions, established by the savings institution's board of directors and included in the savings account contract, that are applicable to each deposit account classification, such as time and amount of deposit, rate of interest, penalty provisions and the account designation.

S

safe deposit box A space in a vault that is rented to an individual for the safekeeping of valuables.

SAIF *See* Savings Association Insurance Fund.

sale leaseback An agreement under which a seller deeds real property to a buyer for a consideration and the buyer then leases the property back to the seller, usually on a long-term basis.

sale and servicing agreement A contract, in secondary market transactions, under which the seller-servicer agrees to supply, and the buyer to purchase, loans from time to time; the contract sets forth the conditions for individual transactions, and the rights and responsibilities of both parties.

Sallie Mae *See* Student Loan Marketing Association.

satisfaction of mortgage A recordable instrument prepared by the lender that evidences payment in full of the mortgage debt. Also known as a release deed.

savings account loan A loan secured by the pledging of savings funds on deposit with the institution.

savings association A financial intermediary that accepts savings from the public and invests those savings mainly in residential mortgage loans; always a corporation, it may be either a mutual or capital stock institution and may be either state-chartered or federally chartered. Also called a savings and loan association, co-operative bank, homestead society, or building and loan association. In this *Glossary*, savings associations are among those businesses referred to as savings institutions.

Savings Association Insurance Fund (SAIF) A fund that insures deposits in Federal Home Loan Bank System member savings associations and other qualifying financial institutions and that is administered by the Federal Deposit Insurance Corporation (FDIC). SAIF is the subfund of the FDIC that continues the insurance coverage for deposits that, prior to FIRREA, were covered by the Federal Savings and Loan Insurance Corporation (FSLIC). *See also* FDIC; BIF; FIRREA.

savings certificate The evidence of ownership of a savings account that typically represents a fixed amount of funds deposited for a fixed term.

savings deposit A deposit for which an institution reserves (but typically does not invoke) the right to require at least seven days' written notice prior to withdrawal or transfer of any funds from the account. Also known as a time deposit. Institutions are permitted to pay interest on NOW accounts, MMDAs, and savings deposits. *See also* demand deposit and time deposit.

R

S

seasoned loan   A loan that has been on the institution's books long enough to demonstrate the borrower's intent to repay the debt.

second mortgage   *See* junior lien.

secondary market   The market through which investments originally sold in the primary market are bought and sold by subsequent owners and purchasers, either over-the-counter or through an exchange.

secondary mortgage market   A market in which mortgage whole loans and interests in blocks of mortgages are bought, sold and traded to other lenders, government agencies or investors.

secured loan   A loan for which the borrower pledges collateral that will be forfeited to the lender in case of default on the loan.

Securities and Exchange Commission (SEC)   A federal commission that has broad regulatory responsibilities over the securities markets, the self-regulatory organizations within the securities industry and persons conducting a business in securities.

Securities Investor Protection Corporation (SIPC)   A nonprofit brokerage community corporation created by an act of Congress to promote investor confidence in the nation's securities markets. It provides protection against theft and loss of securities held only in a brokerage account. The SIPC does not protect against bad investment decisions, bond coupons that were not clipped by mistake or lost interest. Protection is $500,000 per customer of which no more than $100,000 can be used for cash claims.

securities market   A mechanism for the buying and selling of securities between investors; examples are the over-the-counter markets, New York Stock Exchange and American Stock Exchange.

securitization   The pooling of similar loans in a package, which is then sold as a tradable security. The pooling of loans acts as collateral for the securities.

security   1. An evidence of debt or of property (such as a bond or stock certificate). **2.** An item given as a pledge of repayment. **3.** The steps taken by a business to safeguard its offices against theft or vandalism.

security agreement   The section of a note, or a separate document, that represents a transfer of property from a borrower to a creditor, given in fulfillment or satisfaction of a debt. In general, a security agreement identifies the creditor and borrower and contains a description of the collateral. In addition, the terms and conditions of the agreement and any special provisions required by state or federal statutes are listed.

security interest   An interest in collateral that secures payment or performance of an obligation.

SEP   *See* Simplified Employee Pension Plan.

Series EE Bond   An interest-bearing certificate of debt issued at discount by the United States Treasury and sold in denominations of from $50 to $1,000. The bond is redeemable at face value upon maturity. This bond replaced the Series E Bond in 1980. *See also* United States Savings Bond.

Series HH Bond   An interest-bearing certificate of debt issued at par value by the United States Treasury and sold in denominations of $500, $1,000 and $5,000. The owner receives a series of interest payments during the life of the bond. This bond replaced the Series H Bond in 1980. *See also* United States Savings Bond.

service bureau   A business that rents computer time or sells data processing services to users.

service corporation   A corporation, owned by one or more savings institutions, that performs services and engages in certain activities for its owners, such as originating, holding, selling and servicing mortgages; performing appraisal, brokerage, clerical, escrow, research and other services; and acquiring, developing or renovating, and holding real estate for investment purposes.

servicing   *See* loan servicing.

servicing contract   A document, in secondary market transactions, that details servicing requirements and legally binds the servicing institution to carry out the requirements.

settlement statement   *See* loan settlement statement.

settling   The process of balancing the accepted in-clearing drafts and the return items that an institution receives and making the payment within the check collection system.

settlor   A person who makes a settlement or creates a trust of property; also called a grantor.

sight draft   A customer's order to a financial institution holding his or her funds to pay all or part of them to another institution in which the customer holds an account; also called a customer draft.

signature card   A form, executed by a depositor when the depositor opens an account, establishing the type of account ownership and setting forth some of the basic terms of the account.

simple interest   A method of calculating interest in which the amount of the interest is computed on the principal balance of a loan or deposit account for each given period.

S

73

Simplified Employee Pension (SEP) Plan A plan used by an employer to make contributions toward an employee's retirement income. The employer makes contributions, up to annual contribution limits, directly to an Individual Retirement Account set up by an employee with a savings institution, insurance company or other qualified financial institution. *See also* IRA.

single premium life A type of permanent life insurance that can be paid for in one payment. The cash value is usually higher and the death benefit lower than in conventional annual premium policies.

site value The worth of land without improvements, as if vacant.

skiptracing A process in which collectors try to uncover information to help them locate missing debtors and collect repayment.

Small Business Administration (SBA) A federal government agency that makes, guarantees and purchases participations in loans to wholesale, retail, service and manufacturing businesses.

SMSA *See* metropolitan statistical area.

sold loan A mortgage loan that has been sold to an investor but still is serviced by the seller.

source document A financial institution's original written record of a transaction, showing a description of the transaction and authority for making the transaction. Source documents are executed by customers, employees or officers, depending on the type of transaction involved.

sources and uses of funds statement The financial statement that shows the cash flow between balance sheet accounts during a reporting period.

special assessment A claim against a property that arises when the cost of a major improvement, such as street lighting, is distributed among the benefited properties; also called an improvement lien. Failure to pay any installment of the assessment may result in foreclosure by the political entity that levied it.

special endorsement An endorsement that transfers title to a negotiable instrument to a party specified in the endorsement. *See also* blank endorsement; endorsement.

speculate The action of making an investment, despite great uncertainty, in the hope of realizing a substantial return.

split-rate account A special classification on which earnings are paid at more than one rate.

spousal IRA A type of contributory IRA that enables a working spouse to establish an IRA for his or her nonworking spouse. Spousal IRAs were created by the Tax Reform Act of 1976. *See also* IRA.

spread The difference between the return on investments and the cost of funds. *See also* margin.

stale-dated check A check payable on demand that is uncashed for an unreasonable length of time after its issue.

standard consolidated statistical area (SCSA) *See* consolidated metropolitan statistical area.

standard metropolitan statistical area (SMSA) *See* metropolitan statistical area.

standby commitment A promise to loan funds at specific terms in the future if, at that time, the borrower still wants the loan.

statement of changes in financial position A financial statement that outlines the sources and uses of funds and explains changes in cash or working capital of a firm.

statement of condition *See* balance sheet.

statement of operations A financial statement that reports an institution's income and expenses over a specified period.

statement of retained earnings The financial statement of a stock institution that contains a report on the beginning balance of retained earnings, the net income and the withdrawals of the period, and the resulting ending balance of retained earnings. For mutual institutions, this statement is usually called a statement of general reserves.

statement savings A system of reporting on the status of an account. The statement is mailed to the customer at specified periods, and contains a record of any account action—deposits, withdrawals, interest payments, etc.—that has taken place during that period.

statutory right of redemption A defaulted borrower's right, in certain states, to redeem his or her property for a specified period of time after a foreclosure sale, by paying off the debts in default. *See also* equitable right of redemption; redemption right.

stock A certificate in evidence of a shareholder's proportionate ownership of a corporation. The owner may have voting rights and rights to any dividends declared by the board of directors. Also called guaranty stock. *See also* common stock; preferred stock.

S

stock institution   A savings institution organized as a capital stock corporation, with investors providing operating capital by purchasing an ownership interest in the institution, represented by shares of stock. Their stock holdings entitle them to virtually the same rights as stockholders in any other corporation, including a share of the profits.

stock dividend   The distribution of shares of stock in direct proportion to the number of shares originally held by the stockholders of a corporation.

stockholder   A person who owns part of a corporation as represented by the shares held.

stop-payment order   An order by the customer instructing the financial institution to refuse payment of a specific draft or check.

straight-line depreciation method   A systematic conversion of an asset's cost into a periodic expense whereby an equal allocation of original cost is expensed each period of an asset's useful life.

Student Loan Marketing Association (SLMA)   A government-sponsored corporation chartered by Congress to market loans made under the federally sponsored Guaranteed Student Loan Program by financial and education institutions, state agencies and other organizations. It provides a source of funds and a secondary market for government-guaranteed student loans. Also known as Sallie Mae.

subordination clause   A mortgage clause that makes other debts or rights in the real estate secondary to the mortgage.

sum-of-the-years' digits depreciation method   A systematic conversion of an asset's cost into a periodic expense whereby a declining percentage rate is applied to the fixed, depreciable cost of the asset.

Super NOW   A variation of the NOW account. Although the Super NOW has no legal minimum balance or interest rate restrictions, offering institutions typically require a higher minimum balance and pay a higher interest rate than for their NOW accounts. *See also* NOW account.

supervisory authority   The official or officials authorized by law to see that financial institutions are operated in conformity with the charter, statutes, regulations and bylaws governing their operation.

surrender of collateral statement   The statement in a loan contract that gives the lending institution the right to secure personal property without a court order.

survey   A scaled plan drawing that shows the exact dimensions and boundaries of a property, including lot lines and placement of improvements on the property, as well as any easements, rights-of-way or other pertinent information. A survey looks much like a map of the property.

sweep   An arrangement linking an account that pays low interest or no interest (Account A) with an account that pays higher interest (Account B). When the balance in Account A exceeds a specified amount, excess funds are swept into Account B. Conversely, if the balance in Account A falls below a specified amount, money is pulled back into it from Account B.

syndicate   A temporary association of two or more persons formed to carry out some specific business venture. One example is the formation of a syndicate to develop large-scale real estate projects.

system security   The protection of information-system hardware, software and data from unacceptable risks. System security guards against unauthorized access to information and systems and protects the accuracy of the organization's information.

systems analysis   **1.** A detailed examination of the components and requirements of an existing system, such as an organization or a data-processing system. **2.** A detailed examination of the information needs of an organization, the characteristics and components of present information systems, and the data-processing requirements of proposed information systems.

S

T

tax deductions   The expenditures, as allowed by the IRS, that reduce the amount of taxable income; for example, medical expenses, charitable donations and interest paid.

tax-deferred annuity   An investment vehicle in which pretax dollars are invested by an individual to provide a future stream of income to the individual for a definite period of time, or for life. Federal income tax on pretax dollars and interest earned are postponed; generally used for retirement purposes.

tax-deferred income   The income upon which tax liability originates (is established) but income tax payment on this income amount is postponed.

tax-deferred investment   An investment on which the payment of income tax owed is postponed until a later time, usually when a person is in a lower tax bracket.

tax-exempt   An investment that is not subject to federal and/or state income tax.

tax identification number (TIN)   The number used to identify an individual or entity for federal income tax purposes.

tax lien   A government claim against real property for unpaid taxes.

taxable year   The yearly period used as the basis of federal income tax calculations; also known as the tax year. *See also* leeway period.

tax-sheltered income   The total amount of tax-deferred and tax-exempt income earned in a given taxable year. The result is reduced tax liability in the particular taxable year.

tenancy by the entirety   A form of ownership by husband and wife, recognized in certain states, in which the rights of the deceased spouse automatically pass to the survivor.

tenancy in common   A form of ownership in which two or more parties own property, but in which each owns a separate interest; when one owner dies, that owner's share passes to his or her heirs, not to the remaining owner(s). In tenancy in common account ownership, signatures of all owners are necessary for withdrawal.

tenant   A person or business that has the temporary use and right of occupation of real property owned by another.

term   The time period granted for repayment of a loan.

term deposit   *See* time deposit.

term life insurance   A type of life insurance that provides only a death benefit to be paid to a designated beneficiary upon the insurer's death. In general, there is no cash value feature, and coverage terminates at the end of the specified term.

term loan   A loan with a maturity of usually three to five years during which interest is paid but the principal is not reduced. The entire principal is due and payable at the end of its term.

testamentary account   The funds owned and controlled by an individual and invested in a revocable trust account, tentative or Totten Trust account, payable-on-death account or similar account evidencing the intention that funds will be paid to a named party at the owner's death.

third-party sponsored IRA   A trust created by an employer for the exclusive benefit of his or her employees or their beneficiaries or by an association of employees for the exclusive benefit of its members or their beneficiaries and treated as an Individual Retirement Account. *See also* IRA.

thrift institution   A financial intermediary that promotes thrift by providing customers with savings deposit facilities; for example, savings associations, savings banks and credit unions.

tiered-rate account   A special classification on which earnings may be paid at different rates depending upon the balance.

time deposit   A deposit of funds in a savings institution that may be withdrawn under stated conditions as to the time or notice required; also called term deposit.

time share ownership   A form of ownership of real property. Title to a resort or vacation home is divided among many different owners. Each owner acquires the right to occupy the property during a specified portion of each year.

time-sharing   A data-processing operation in which a computer is shared by several users working at separate terminals at the same time.

TIN   *See* tax identification number

title   The ownership right to property including the right to possession. *See also* abstract of title.

title insurance   The insurance which protects the lender and the homeowner against loss resulting from any defects in the title or claims against a property that were not uncovered in the title search and that are not specifically listed as exemptions to the coverage on the title insurance policy.

Title I   The section of the National Housing Act of 1934 that authorizes the Federal Housing Administration to insure home improvement and mobile home loans.

title report   A written statement by a title company of the condition of title to a particular piece of real estate as of a certain date.

title search   A review of public records to disclose any claims or defects in the current owner's title to real estate.

Title II   The section of the National Housing Act of 1934 that covers all basic residential mortgage insurance programs of the Federal Housing Administration.

tolerance range   An accurate calculation of the annual percentage rate (APR) to within ranges prescribed by federal regulations. Depending on the transaction type, the APR must be within either ⅛ or ¼ of 1% of the figures computed by the federal examiner.

Totten Trust   A revocable trust account established without a written trust agreement.

town house   A low-rise, single-family dwelling attached to two or more similar dwellings separated by party walls and having separate entrances.

trailing edge of a check   The left-hand edge of a check's printed side.

transaction   An event that causes some change in the assets, liabilities or net worth of a business.

transaction account   A deposit account that permits the account holder to make payments or transfers to a third party. Such payments or transfers may be made by check, negotiable order of withdrawal (NOW accounts), telephone transfer, automated teller machine or other electronic devices. *See also* demand deposit; Federal funds interest rate; Regulation D.

transit number   An identifying code number devised by the American Bankers Association and assigned to each financial institution in the check-clearing system. Each number has two parts, separated by a hyphen. The first part is a code identifying the geographic location of the paying institution; the second part is a code identifying the institution itself.

traveler's check   An order, over the signature of the issuing company, to pay on demand the amount shown by the denomination of the check. Traveler's checks may be cashed almost anywhere in the world and are insured against loss, theft and destruction. *See also* check.

Treasury bill   A short-term Treasury obligation issued at a discount under competitive bidding, with a maturity of up to one year. It is issued payable to the bearer only, and is not sold in amounts of less than $10,000.

Treasury bond A federal government obligation, ordinarily payable to the bearer, that is issued at par, with maturities of more than five years and interest payable semiannually.

Treasury certificate A United States security usually issued at par, with a specified rate of interest and a maturity of one year or less; issued payable to the bearer and not sold in amounts of less than $1,000.

Treasury note An obligation of the United States, usually issued payable to the bearer, with a fixed maturity of not less than one year or more than 10 years; issued at par, with a specified semiannual interest return.

truncation *See* check truncation.

trust A completed transfer of ownership of a piece of property by the owner (grantor) to another (the trustee) for the immediate or eventual benefit of a third person (the beneficiary). *See also* custodial IRA.

trust account **1.** A deposit account, established under a trust arrangement, that contains funds administered by a trustee for the benefit of another person or persons. **2.** An escrow account. *See also* irrevocable trust; revocable trust.

trust agreement A written agreement under which a grantor transfers legal ownership of property to another person or entity for the benefit of a third person subject to the various incidents of a trust.

trustee The legal title holder and controller of funds in a trust account established for the benefit of another according to a trust agreement.

trust fund A financial arrangement in which financial resources are placed in the custody of an individual (trustee) by someone (grantor) for the benefit of another person (beneficiary). One person may fill more than one role, depending on the type of trust.

trust indenture *See* deed of trust.

Truth-in-Lending Act The popular name for the Consumer Credit Protection Act of 1968 and its provisions that require lenders to make certain disclosures of financing costs to the borrower at specified times in the loan application process. *See also* Regulation Z.

turnkey program A United States Department of Housing and Urban Development program for public housing whereby, under contract to a local housing authority, a private developer builds public housing with private loan funds and, upon completion of the project, turns over to the housing authority the keys to the property.

203(b) loan A home mortgage loan insured by the Federal Housing Administration under Section 203(b) of the National Housing Act of 1934.

U

uncollected funds   The funds that have been deposited in an account from a check that has not yet been paid by the drawee bank.

underwriting   The process, in mortgage lending, of determining the risks inherent in a particular loan and establishing suitable loan terms and conditions. Underwriting also includes the process of evaluating a loan applicant's ability and willingness to repay a loan.

unearned interest   The interest on a loan that has already been collected but has not yet been earned because the principal has not been outstanding long enough.

Uniform Commercial Code   A body of business-related laws dealing with sale of goods, their transportation and delivery, financing, storage and final payment.

Uniform Settlement Statement   The Department of Housing and Urban Development form that lists all charges imposed on the borrower and the seller in connection with a home mortgage loan settlement. The Real Estate Settlement Procedures Act requires that the lender make the Statement available to the buyer and seller at the time of settlement. *See also* Real Estate Settlement Procedures Act.

Uniform Transfers to Minors Act   An act that sets forth provisions for giving a minor an intangible gift (e.g., bank accounts, stocks or bonds), that results in income shifting with an adult serving as custodian. The custodian (e.g., parent) has direct control over the gift and can sell and reinvest proceeds from the gift for the minor with the minor recognizing any gain and/or annual income that results. The minor's income from the gift cannot be combined with the custodian's property (e.g., parents using part of the child's income to purchase a car for the parents). Also called the Uniform Gifts to Minors Act.

unit investment trust   A classification of investment company issuing redeemable securities sold in units that represent the undivided interest in a group of securities, such as mortgages or municipal bonds.

United States Savings Bond   The interest-bearing certificate of debt issued by the United States Treasury. It is nontransferable, noncallable, registered, redeemable at specified redemption values, variable as to time of maturity, and exempt from state and local taxes. *See also* Series EE Bond; Series HH Bond.

universal life   A form of permanent life insurance in which the death benefit may be adjusted up or down and premium payments may vary from year to year.

unqualified opinion   The second paragraph in an independent auditor's report that states that the financial statements present fairly the financial position of a firm according to generally accepted accounting principles applied on a basis consistent with that of the previous year.

unsecured credit   The credit extended on the borrower's promise to repay and for which collateral is not required. It is usually extended to consumers possessing a good credit reputation.

usury   An amount of interest, charged for the use of money, that is more than allowed by law.

U

V

VA *See* Veterans Administration.

valuation An estimated value of real property.

value The dollar amount placed on collateral that indicates the price for which it can be realistically sold.

variable rate certificate A certificate account with an interest rate that fluctuates during the deposit term according to a predetermined schedule and formula index.

vesting The process by which an employee's rights to retirement benefits become nonforfeitable. Most pension or profit-sharing plans allow for vesting to take place in stages, according to a predetermined formula and over a set period of time. In contrast, IRA contributions are vested fully and immediately on a participant's behalf.

Veterans Administration (VA) A government agency that aids veterans of the U.S. armed forces in various ways; its housing assistance takes the form of a guarantee to the financial institution on loans with low downpayments to qualified veterans.

voluntary association account A deposit account held by a nonincorporated group, such as a club, baseball team, church, civic group or charity; otherwise, generally similar to a corporation account.

voucher payment plan A method of construction loan payouts in which the contractor or borrower completes lender forms requesting each payout when a particular, prespecified stage of construction is reached.

W

wage assignment   A written agreement between a borrower and a financial institution, which states that upon default, the institution has the right to obtain a specific portion of the borrower's wages from a specific employer without notice or hearing. Federal regulations prohibit this type of clause in consumer loans and certain equity loans made by Federal Home Loan Bank System members. The wage assignment differs from wage garnishments in that garnishments require a court judgment, whereas assignments do not.

wage garnishment   A legal proceeding whereby a financial institution seeks a court order to obtain debt repayment from a third party (employer) who owes money (wages) to a borrower.

warranty deed   A deed in which the seller warrants that the title to the real estate is good, merchantable and without defects.

whole loan   A mortgage loan sold in its entirety by the original lender to an investor. When a whole loan is sold, all of the contractual rights and responsibilities of the original lender pass to the investor.

wholesale banking   The function of providing bank services, loan security and loans to large corporate customers.

withdrawal form   A source document and authorization for withdrawals from a savings account used by the customers and kept by the savings institution for its records.

withdrawal ratio   The ratio of withdrawals expressed as a percentage of gross savings receipts for a given period of time.

with full recourse   A term in a written agreement, used in lending, that gives the buyer in a sale or other transaction the right to full reimbursement from the seller for any losses resulting from the loans or other items purchased.

withholding   The amount deducted from gross wages or other taxable income at the time of receipt.

without recourse   A term in a written agreement, used in lending, that abrogates the right of the buyer, in a sale or other transaction, to reimbursement from the seller for any subsequent losses resulting from the loans or other items purchased.

with partial recourse   A term in a written agreement, used in lending, that gives the buyer in a sale or other transaction the right to reimbursement for an agreed-upon portion of any losses resulting from the loans or other items purchased.

85

wraparound mortgage   A mortgage loan that secures a debt that includes the balance due on an existing senior mortgage loan and an additional amount advanced by the wraparound lender. The wraparound lender thereafter makes the amortizing payments on the senior mortgage.

write-off   The accounting procedure of removing an amount from the asset category of a balance sheet and recording it as an expense item on the income statement; this type of adjustment is necessary when an institution takes a loss, as in the sale of real estate owned.

Y

yield The return on an investment, expressed as a percentage of the market price or, where the investment is owned, of the price paid for it originally. *See also* effective yield; rate of return.

yield curve A line or curve that graphically represents the relationship between interest rates of securities having equal qualities but different maturities.

yield interest rate The actual rate of return an investor receives on an investment.

yield to maturity A yield concept designed to give the investor the average annual yield on a security. This calculation is based on the interest rate, price and length of time to maturity; and takes into account any bond premium or discount.

Z

zero-coupon bond A debt issue with no coupons that promises to pay face value at a designated future date, usually 10 years hence. Interest accrues and is taxable, but not paid until redemption. It is sold at a substantial discount.

zoning ordinance A community law designed to classify and regulate land use, in order to protect the health, welfare and safety of people in the community.